EARLY REVIEW FOR SOUL STORIES: NINE PASSAGES OF INITIATION

In *Soul Stories,* Gail Burkett has created a guide that will deeply affect the lives of whoever decides to pick it up. These stories of passages and initiations create new understanding, awareness, honor and respect for all that we have been, are now and are becoming. I don't know why these stories and initiations well up sadly sweet tears … this must be the missing piece in our culture. Thank you so much for sharing this wise, ripe gift!

-Nancy Smith, Fine Arts and Education Advocate, College of Idaho

Soul Stories is a tool for all of us to learn and reflect on our own Passages. The Life Spiral is an important reminder that our birth years may not account for the entire picture of our lives and we certainly can use "humor to adapt to these times." I find rituals to be part of our daily life; we just don't recognize them. *Soul Stories* can teach us to recognize and honor our rituals, open ourselves up to new rituals that will help us to adapt, honor our past, yet live in the present moment.

-Michele Burkett, Realtor, Wilderness Advocate

In *Soul Stories* Gail Burkett invites women, gently and persistently, to listen to our souls, to find out who we are and how our journey through life has brought us to this now moment - a moment to be celebrated. Follow this guide and the callings of your own heart and you will harvest the wisdom of your stories, the beauty of your changes as you moved through life, and a deep knowing of who you truly are. You will not be disappointed.

-Lorene Wapotich, M.Ed., Founder & Executive Director,
Feet on the Earth Programs

Thank you Gail! for this beautiful book, for allowing these rites to flow through you with courage and passion. *Soul Stories* is written in a way that will help any woman heal the hurts of the past and grow into a grand future. You're paving the way for all of us, from grandmas to our baby girls. I will be sending this book to every woman I love and many women that I know.

-Deborah Gift, Shamanic Practitioner

Soul Stories charts a way through the maze of our lives through Rites of Passage rituals and ceremonies. It stirs a curiosity to ask ourself "Who am I and who was I born to be?" Through reflection, ceremonies, rituals and Rites of Passages, Gail leads us to drop our cloaks and embrace the One We Are, with a new understanding of self and the importance of Rites Of Passage ceremonies in our culture!

-Kathleen Bjorkman Wilson, Rites of Passage and Wilderness Guide

These days there is a rising awareness of conscious elderhood. In *Soul Stories: Nine Passages of Initiation*, Gail Burkett brings forth a guide for claiming all our Rites of Passage and stepping into the elder stage of life with conscious intent, grace, and renewed purpose. Whether you are age 20 or 100, *Soul Stories* offers you a loom upon which to weave the Soul tapestry of your life. Thank you, Gail, for your inspired vision and passion to birth this guidebook.

-**Reverend Arianna S. Husband, Spiritual Guide and Mentor, Rites of Passage**

The weaving of one's actions towards one person or another, one book or another can be a Mystery. By joining the circle with Gail Burkett, author of *Soul Stories: Nine Passages of Initiation*, and six other women, we were woven together in poetry, in song, in moon cycles all within our life stories. I had a passion to weave the tapestry of my Elder garment by listening to those who had explored this territory before me, sharing what they discovered. Each initiatory threshold brings an anchor and a gift that carries a brighter light into whatever you now choose for your life.

-**Reverend Judith Lay, Spiritual Elder**

Gail Burkett is an initiated Elder whose life purpose is to bring ritual, recognition and respect to every women across the thresholds of time through Rites of Passage. In *Soul Stories: Nine Passages of Initiation*, Gail presents her Coyote questions to challenge memory and restore Soul parts lost upon the trail.

Janis Monaco Clark, Editor, The Flowerlover

As an elder woman who has walked, dreamed, lived and loved through ritual and ceremony, *Soul Stories* gifts each of us through our feminine ways many paths and questions to peek or dive deeply into past memories. From this ever evolving interactive guide, take this "sacred time" to experience with honor and grace your personal lifetime of stories with new eyes and heart wide open.

-**Gail Daehlin**

Books by this Author:

Gifts from the Elders: Girls' Path to Womanhood

Girls' Ceremonies of Nine Passages, Kindle Edition

Soul Stories

Nine Passages of Initiation

I wish you a joyous journey!

Gail Burkett

Gail Burkett, PhD

**TURTLE
MOON
PUBLISHING**

Soul Stories: Nine Passages of Initiation

Inquiries regarding requests to reprint or reproduce any or all of Soul Stories: Nine Passages of Initiation should be directed to the publisher, TurtleMoon Publishing.

TurtleMoon Publishing
310 Grouse Creek Road
Sandpoint, Idaho 83864

TurtleMoon Publishing promotes ritual and ceremony as Women's Way to inhabit the 21st Century. All works advocate for women and girls.

Library of Congress registration pending

First Edition

Print ISBN 978-0-9913590-1-1

PDF e-book ISBN 978-0-9913590-2-8
Kindle ISBN 978-0-9913590-3-5

Design: Laura Wahl
Editor: Janis Monaco Clark
Ceremony photos by Mason White

DEDICATION WITH GREAT LOVE

I dedicate this book to Shirley Hardy who was my wise Spiritual Elder when I went through all the doorways that led to my Elder Encore. In a magnificent way, Shirley demonstrated a threshold crossing into the stage beyond Elder called Spiritual Elder. I promise to tell your story in a good way, Dear Friend, in Nine Passages. Thank you for being you.

I dedicate this book to 3Beauties—Julia Zalesak, Kimberlie Gridley, and Sophia Rubedo—you took me along on your journey to recover Rites of Passage for yourselves, bravely, wholeheartedly, and at the tender age of 35.

Deep personal explorations of another group immediately followed, including me. We are the newly initiated Elders. I hold these Soul Stories tenderly and wholeheartedly: Janis Monaco Clark, Arianna Husband, Kit Kincaid, Judith Lay, Laura Wahl, and Kay Walker. We have revealed ourselves and our gifts to ourselves; the flowering we all found beneath our armor has shown every one of our stories to be precious.

Each of you have helped me create this mystical path for all women to follow, especially women between 30 and 100.

Table of Contents

INTRODUCTION: GUIDE FOR PASSAGES   11
ORIENTATION: Remember Your Soul Story   15
    Crowning for Elders, the Way There   17
    Turning the Focus to You   20

ENTERING   23
    Reviewing the Spiral   28
    Four Rituals to Make Your Own   33
    Other Luminaries   43
    Begin with Care   49
    Womb to Birth Threshold   51
    Birth Threshold   59
    Middle Child Threshold   67
    First Blood Threshold   75
    First Flight Threshold   91
    Womanhood Bloom Threshold   108
    Deepening Womanhood Threshold   119
    Elder Encore Threshold   132
    Spiritual Elder Threshold   138
Epilog   140

STORIES FROM SOUL SISTERS   142
    The Story Began with 3Beauties   185

Acknowledgements   198

Author Biography   201

Dear Reader,

Life has a way of offering pure synchronicity when your youthful heart wants to reconnect to the magic in your Soul. If you have passed through your Child and Adolescent years, and you are somewhere between 30 and 100 on your timeline, you may be ready to receive this gift. In honor of the work you have done to be here, now, I bow deeply to you. You have sculpted yourself through trainings, readings, and life lived. Allow me to wrap you in my esteem as the smartest woman I know. This is how synchronicity works.

I am here as your Rites of Passage Guide and Elder Mentor encouraging you to remember your stories and to recover pieces of your Soul left behind on the path of your life. This is a pilgrimage to begin at the beginning, before your Birth, to experience the Passage thresholds that evolved you. When you focus on the healing inner light of your heart-mind, you will recover every one of the catalysts of change to cross five, six, or seven thresholds; then you will better understand ritual, ceremony, celebration, and healing. Throughout this journey, I talk about your Genius and Soul as interchangeable energies of inspiration, intuition, and your connection to Source, the God of your understanding.

This, my dear reader, is our collective way as women to change our culture. When you move around the seasons of a year, you will gain a new understanding of your family members. Their own Souls may desire this deeper conversation because the catalyst of change is in them as it is in you. Taking this pilgrimage back through your life will be profoundly in service to yourself first and bring your legacy into stark relief. With your deeply personal understanding of Passages, the ordeals leading up to them, and the high ritual of crossing these thresholds, you will prepare yourself to lead others. You will become an initiated Elder. Another guidebook called *Nine Passages* to assist you to lead others will be released at the end of the year. I offer *Soul Stories* for your spiritual journey to yourself, first.

Disclaimer: I must be honest and add this caveat before you see your journey ahead as one sweet, little time capsule for the next 9 or 12 months. This pilgrimage remembers the sacred descents you took in your life and all of your ecstatic peaks. My own Soul pieces were sliced off in not-so-nice compromises; those feelings of oppression dragged me down. I went to talking therapy and came out the other side much relieved. You already know some of the terrain ahead. Big healing is possible in this pilgrimage to recover, reclaim, and come to new terms with your memories.

Gail Burkett
March 26, 2015

Raven at Solstice by Marilyn McIntyre

INTRODUCTION: GUIDE FOR PASSAGES

Ponder this: "If gratitude is a state of being that is essential to a life well lived, why then do we not cultivate and express it on a daily basis?"[2]

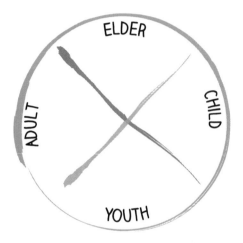

When you cut a circle into four equal slices—Child, Youth, Adult, and Elder—each appears as an equal slice. This is purely metaphoric because the days lived in each slice are not equal. My model of Nine Passages around the Life Spiral emerges out of observation of human ecology within our culture. Common to every human, two developmental stages—early and late—within each quadrant are worth noticing and celebrating. This vision gives rise to gratitude.

You have a great healing and awakening waiting for you in this Elder initiation guide. Elder is not just my word for the arc of life beyond adulthood, it is an honored and a wholehearted embrace of maturity. In our midst, people are dying as adolescents having never evolved their adulthood and old adults are dying who never embraced their elderhood. These Souls have been arrested in their development and secretly hold their misery. For you to participate in the maturity of our culture, initiation will bring you the great satisfaction of completion for nearly every life stage and relief will wrap you in the honoring shawl of an Elder. You will be the model for three generations coming up, the unborn, the youth and the adults who look to you for the sculpting of their own life purpose and for answers about the mysteries of life.

Soul Stories emerges out of that weave as my gift to my peers. I assume only one thing, if you are a Baby Boomer you have accumulated many stories worth remembering, collecting, and sharing. Taking this journey alone—or with a circle of women—will heal you, to your core.

If Rites of Passage ceremonies are to return to our culture, we need to sift through the dust of our Ancestors to discover how the old ways might marry new ways. Only a few of the old ways have been found, we have nothing more than a platform. We all stand on the shoulders of those who have preserved the social structure for initiations.[3] To grow more mature as a culture, initiated Elders need to lead the way, teaching the three younger generations about honoring their Rites of Passage journeys and thresholds of change.

Initiated Elders are needed to encourage the process of evolution for ourselves and our culture. In women's gatherings, I watch and listen for the Elder's voice. Through sharing food, fire, and ambience, trust is the single most powerful element that encourages that confident voice to venture out. With trust, women create a force for good, but without trust, we remain small, sheltering ourselves. Relationships offer the best platform for sharing and for healing; deeper bonds are created when risk and trust create a foundation for our collective voices. Initiating in small groups will provide the trust, develop the relationships, and free the voices of evolving women. Us first, then our girls; men and boys will be next. Awakened women are walking gold mines for others, our stories matter. We offer humor and hope, we understand pain and disappointment, younger women and girls only need us to be authentic and generous. In giving we receive.

I would like to turn the light your way, hear your voice, laugh and cry with you. More than anything in the world, I would like to honor you with an initiation to elevate your status to Elder. When you go on this pilgrimage to yourself, you will learn about Passages and rituals, you will be both creative and deeply quiet in this process and your life will make sense. Bring a few other women into your circle, become Soul Sisters and prepare for the most glorious year of your life. This journey will be the launch-pad for your thrilling Elder years ahead.

I welcome Sue Monk Kidd's concept of telling our stories to other women. In such abundance, good women with good stories and ideas, inspires me to celebrate. I will light a candle and we can begin. In *The Dance of the Dissident Daughter*, Sue Monk Kidd has written to our common heart:

"The truth is, in order to heal we need to tell our stories and have them witnessed ... The story itself becomes a vessel that holds us up, that sustains, that allows us to order our jumbled experiences into meaning.

As I told my stories of fear, awakening, struggle, and transformation and had them received, heard, and validated by other women, I found healing. I also needed to hear other women's stories in order to see and embrace my own. Sometimes another woman's story becomes a mirror that shows me a self I haven't seen before. When I listen to her tell it, her experience quickens and clarifies my own. Her questions rouse mine. Her conflicts illumine my conflicts. Her resolutions call forth my hope. Her strengths summon my strengths. All of this can happen even when our stories and our lives are very different." [1]

ORIENTATION: Remember your Soul Story

We have a whole story, you and I, but do you feel whole? Your story will reveal patterns, fates, and pure luck—both good and bad—when you begin this Soul search.

Soul Stories will serve as a spiritual counselor to help recover the Soul of your story. Soul is and has been patient, but as your most essential companion, your Soul may need this pilgrimage to recover all parts of your wholeness. You may adopt this guide as counselor to open your inner eyes as to how growth moved you through the stages between each of the Passages of your life. Your imagination and memory will serve you best. *Soul Stories* helps remove blockages and recover lost parts of Soul.

To reintroduce Rites of Passage into the culture I see old ways needing to marry with new. We call on the old ways as we can find them through stories. When offered Elder-to-younger, Passage rituals, drawn from old ways when story was shared orally, followed this pattern—hearing the call, separating oneself, crossing a threshold, enduring some test or ordeal, shedding an old skin to experience a small death, and returning to share one's story with community as a changed person with a new identity. Members of the community who witnessed the leaving and the returning reflected the changes and reinforced them to fully develop the next level of maturity.

Here's where I enter a lament: If only there were more initiated Elders, if only our community consciousness included how

Passage rituals lead to healing, to wholeness, and to tending our Souls. If only adults, new and old, would step into a Rites of Passage space, consciousness would shift all around the planet. Old-old ways need to be respected for their deep wisdom. For spaciousness to be created revealing the next level of maturity, separation and a challenge provide the psychic fuel. During a small death ritual, Soul emerges with both hands clapping; let go, release the old, the next stage will reveal more of your gifts. The pattern is a good one. I ask for more initiated Elders to stand beside me and help update the ancient ways for the 21st Century. I am writing to cure this lament felt by many.

How have the natural developmental stages moved through you and which Passages have you missed celebrating? When we entered initiation, my friends and I called it double-tracking. The foundation stones of childhood are difficult to remember, but they include good manners, right and wrong behavior, social courtesies, holidays and birthday parties. The girl you were at 10, at 20 and the woman you became at 30, all of your former personae still live inside. By looking back and within, you will discover how often your Soul has whispered through your life. This pilgrimage will begin before Birth and slowly track forward to remember your spirit's journey through all the days of your life. Your precious Soul gifts will slowly re-emerge.

Crowning for Elders, the Way There

This may be the only time you have ever considered your Soul as a thing to talk about, but why are you here? When your rowdy spirit quiets down to the Earth and you spend sweet time in Nature where spirits from other realms feel inclined to visit, you open to your Soul-self. Discovering profound quiet in Nature allows you to focus attention on your Soul's story as a subject to love. This Soul-full pilgrimage revisits the stories along your spirit trail looking for the markers of maturity since your Birth. With no concept of time, Soul fulfillment has waited patiently for you. Rites of Passage is Soul work, revealing yourself to yourself.[3]

This guide is designed to recover your Passage ceremonies. One by one, a ceremony will be created for each threshold while you double-track in your life. On one track, do what you always do. Then add a sacred dimension to your life and your personal ecological space for ritual and ceremony. This track of wonder floats above and within. When you begin, give the story of your womb-time special attention while you do dishes, or make the bed, or do your laundry. Double-track refers to a thought process, an immersion, while the rest of your life also carries on. When you have time to write or journal, you add that in as it fits.

The task of this journey will require ten minutes most days. Immersion is what your psyche longs for. This is key. You do a normal routine—personal and family agendas—while you also hold aloof, ever so lightly, a story practice to re-inform each one of your life stages in growth order. You have become skilled enough for autopilot of the mundane. Like wrapping yourself in a bubble with your Soul-self, double-tracking circles back through the turning of the Earth as you grew through each season. Your prize will be a new vision of who you are today.

Immersion into the sacred memories of your past days will inform in all new ways and new perspectives as you dedicate your days to Divine witness. As you put your mind on every birthday and significant event along your timeline, those memories will trigger significant moments and more memories.

Once you step your heart and mind through your natural history, you will see, even feel, all the twists of fate that have been working to tack you into the wind of your destiny. You will also recognize how the hand of God or the Divine helped you by sending intuitive and even physical messages. You will find awe as your patterns emerge.

You can and will remember why you are here. Gifts delivered by your Soul when you were born will emerge from behind the shadows. Your Soul will show you places where your primary instructions stick out of your history. Finding or remembering requires a pilgrimage like this to search out your Soul-self. Whenever you feel ready to begin, I am honored to be your guide.

The Life Spiral

I invite you to gaze into the Spiral artwork. Jean Herzel envisioned symbols for the peak moments that mark a woman's development. The Life Spiral is lively and lovely; I adore the symbolism and how it reflects humor to adapt to these times.

This is the time, now, for the celebration of wholeness. This is the time for feeding our woman-spirits. The lifting of women's Passages will soon flow over into men's Passages. Soon every baby, every middle child and every pubescent youth, oh yes and each young woman leaving home, will have a Passage ritual to claim for their very own. More and more Elders will step forward to harvest their Soul bundles through their initiatory fire of transformation. Initiated Elders will discover their Genius steps forward for an encore.

Turning the Focus to You

If you agree that your life, your character, and your imagination could be more aligned with the sacred Divine, if you wished you had received ceremonies to celebrate your life's change markers, if you would like to share Rites of Passage with your friends and family, or if you want the culture to grow up, then *Soul Stories* is especially designed to help you. Before I became a guide and Elder mentor, I turned myself completely inside out several times. Now I can see the sense and the ease of starting at the very beginning, inside the oceanic wonder of the womb.

Living a ritual life is my most dramatic personal transformation and a gift I give my Soul for being so patient with me. Ritual is my gift to the Planet because it brings me to quiet reverence, and quickly. From inside, the deep quiet of reverence teaches me ever more about awareness and caring for my Great Mother, the Earth. My senses feel alive and enliven my Soul-self.

When you crossed through each stage of development, your change was dramatic enough that you almost felt like a different species. In Nature the image is a snake that sheds its dry, scaly old skin; for a time it must feel utterly new and different. How did you move from early to middle childhood, exactly? How did you adapt enough to accept puberty? Your inner experience of operating with an adult brain adjusted and brought new agreements for your body and psyche. You are adaptable!

All through your life, the more you were challenged, the more you adapted, but how were these changes storied in you and in your family? Do you mostly remember the story told about you? What happened when no threshold ritual of welcoming and celebration was experienced? Repeat, disappoint, repeat, disappoint.

Perhaps your Soul created a crisis to move beyond the tension? I learned this about my demanding Soul the hard way and more than once. Spiritual crisis often resolves the tension and temporarily relieves arrested development. Drama can become the only way forward, or worse, perpetual addictions settle in. If you are lucky, moving slowly and going deep to revisit your stages of development, you will discover that each threshold still holds a moment ripe for a long overdue transformation. That transforming energy includes releasing the old self and honoring the ordeal that pushed you to and through your edge of change.

Throughout the next decade, ten thousand Boomers will retire every day. To everyone older than 60 I say, "Welcome to your Elderhood. This is a glorious place from which to view the world. All of your facets coalesce as a gift for giving. I honor you." Think of everything you know and all you have experienced. Just think of how good you feel. Maybe you don't even feel your age, lucky you, but still you are too old to be in denial. You are an Elder and hopefully this wonder-age will last many years! I feel especially grateful for the opportunity to express myself through an Elder Encore, it is a magnificent rebirth. Right now is the time to think about your initiation. The Youngers need us to get ourselves ready.

ENTERING

Find your place along the arc of ages on the Spiral of Life. Begin on the right, in the East place where the Sun rises. Your Birth happened when the planets aligned just so to support your destiny. Growing every day, you moved through Early to Middle Childhood, First Blood, First Flight, and Womanhood with relative oblivious ease, unless like me, a Soul-knocking crisis threw you into change.

To become fully mindful and mellow means finding wholeness. To be initiated to your mature status and in the right place on the Spiral, take yourself with a couple of friends through all the Passages you missed. Enter a liminal space together and experience a sacred remembering through a pilgrimage that began when your Soul flew in from the stars to join that embryonic biology growing in your Mother's womb. This journey examines and reclaims the pebbles left along your spirit trail. You need those Soul parts to be whole.

Pilgrimage Design

To reclaim what is yours make a commitment to begin and end in a good way. Ask three or more kindred spirits to take this journey with you. Who would share your willingness to search out the deepest threads of their memories? Choose willing Soul Sisters, as you may need them to lift you. If you are in your thirties or forties, wanting to catch up to your Womanhood threshold, I recommend a minimum of six months for this double-tracking expedition. You will need one month, at least, to remember the meaningful moments inside of the thousands of days between each threshold. If you are in your fifties, sixties, or seventies, please plan carefully. A year-long spiritual pilgrimage with your circle will go by very fast.

When you feel ready to commit, gather with your journey companions and talk about how you want this spiritual pilgrimage to unfold. There is no rush to begin, choose the wise way to proceed. Enter into a deep quiet with your group by sitting beside a stream or a fire. You might want to sit in a circle in your living room and find Nature's stillness by playing ocean music. When you look into the eyes of your pilgrimage sisters, you know you have common threads even though your inner work remains personal. Call in the energies of the four directions as guardians of all that is sacred, if this is your way. Each woman offers a ritual element: a prayer, a poem, a song, or a drumming chant. To do this holy pilgrimage of remembering, you will follow your God of the inner and outer realms. Since this work is deeply personal, you may weave in religious beliefs or leave them aside. You are the weaver.

The Passages which need to be celebrated after Birth and before you leave home include Middle Child Rites, First Blood, and First Flight. All four Passages built on one another and prepared your young woman-self for the grand experiment, the test of your independence. *Soul Stories* escorts you over each of these thresholds. Remembering will be self-satisfying in surprising ways. Follow this story-line on behalf of your Soul to recover places where shadow parts broke away and other places where clues about your gifts and life purpose were left unattended and abandoned.

If your earliest three ritual Passages have been celebrated, you are a cultural rarity to be honored and we need you to teach us. If not, ask the Ancestors to forgive our audacity for being pioneers for Rites of Passage. This will add spice to your motivating energy, so you may begin in a good way.

Our view of development has been under a microscope for a very long time. Your adult brain began its maturity around age 14, but throughout the whole next decade that brain used training wheels. In a natural spreading of neuro-pathways, your mind began to locate throughout your body. Body-mind is a powerful tool, as an adolescent you learned this, and probably you are still learning. During the second half of adolescence, less coddling happened and the culture battered your very Soul while it was searching for true North. Those training wheels fell away when you were not looking because your brain finally matured around age 25.

The Spiral's Hemispheres

Yes, each stage offers early and late: Child, Youth, Adult, and Elder. When you finally reach adulthood or womanhood, you will remember how and why it took so very long. It's best to have a deeper look into this vast space after the early thresholds have been crossed. Thanks to your wide vision of life, each life development stage holds something remarkably new for you.

As you revisit your life stories, the space between each Passage will be filled in, remembered your unique way. Call forth Soul-listening and learn this new skill. Every Soul is unique. Our work together is transformational. You will find your amazing story waiting to be remembered in all the days between each of your natural, developmental thresholds. Journeys up to the present have been fun-filled and messy with every emotion, but remembering your choices and motivations make your story yours. Your goals and priorities were unique and so are the bodily storage places for your wounds. To support this once in a lifetime pilgrimage, ask your Soul Sisters to spend time in circle, and I recommend before each threshold that you share a talking stick. You may even decide to be together to help one another across some or all of the thresholds ahead. This journey is yours to define.

To grow in relationship with your Soul and your purpose, be very clear about your commitment. Through deep remembering, this pilgrimage holds all the clues to reveal more of yourself to yourself. You will use investigative skills, searching through highs and lows to remember your story. I hope you record your dreams. Perhaps sleeping with mugwort will activate your dreamtime. Maybe your peaks were more than a single moment, with a slow build-up before a crescendo. Perhaps you will experience a slow release into the next phase with no drama. Maybe this long journey will provide valuable notes for writing memoir, but I am sure the focus on your Soul will be sufficient for your commitment to grow stronger along the way.

I am especially interested in sharing how luxurious and rare it feels to revisit each Passage. This work is folk psychology. Think "ology" of the psyche, what does this mean to you? Stories around the central fire, this is the origin of folk psychology now circling back. Story and psychology are folk arts and belong to every single person. At its essence, psychology, the telling of stories, works when it helps reclaim parts of you left behind, pieces of your psyche left hiding in trauma or shadow. Your Soul continually wants answers to questions: what, why, and how. Quests appear as opportunities to discover your truth. Your personal cosmology, your inner truth, seeks the a-ha moments that belong to you alone. This is spiritual reclamation work. If you carry questions about your Soul's purpose, gifts that you brought with you at birth will be more obvious in this deep remembering. To be whole, to embrace your wholeness, you must claim and express your gifts.

REVIEWING THE SPIRAL

Rites of Passage, as an ancient means for encouraging and recognizing transformation, has a language all of its own. In order of occurrence the process includes hearing the call, separating from ordinary life, seeing the threshold and crossing into liminal space. Find peace with not knowing as you enter the liminal spaces between what you know and what you don't know yet. Once inside the shimmer of change, the length of liminal time varies. The little death rituals are for letting go of the past, pain and joy and all, to embrace the new. These ancient and accepted steps are observed for each Passage ahead. It would be helpful to you to keep these steps in mind before you stand in front of each threshold. In reviewing your life for this Elder initiation, you will notice an all new satisfied feeling when you recreate ceremonies so each Passage has its story punctuated with completion.

Womb Time. Gestation is fascinating and the mystery of how you came to be as your father's sperm entered the egg offered by your mother. This time can be drawn or written about while you imagine the story that surrounded your conception.

Birth and Childhood. For the 3000 days of your childhood, photos may help you review playing, crawling, toddling, walking, talking, and running. Your ontogeny produced baby teeth which fell out to leave space to grow in new teeth. These may remind you of more changes; how does the chronicle of your childhood read?

Middle Child. This time belongs to your sweet big-girl from approximately 8 to 13. Your big-girl self offered a magical expression of your true self in body, mind, and character. Your personality developed. What clues emerge from this special time before more hormones flooded your blood stream?

First Blood. Some of us shed 400 eggs in shame and disguise. Women I know would like to change this one thing about our mutual experience. We would create space and time to re-vision life, our pace would be slow, and the essence would be sacred. Remember your whole early teen time. Days, weeks, months were endured to develop your character amidst the upheaval and chaos of your teen experience. Then, you reached an even grander threshold as an eager and confidant young woman.

First Flight. You felt completely ready to enter the fray of life beyond your parent's nest. What was your story? Perhaps you didn't leave. If you take the time to do this mental, emotional, and spiritual work of remembering and reclaiming, all aspects of yourself will weave and blend. Breathe.

I suggest you take a break before you cross the Adult thresholds to prevent your good focus from feeling like work. I call this an eddy, a quiet place for reflection. The very foundation stones for your entire life have been remembered. Go to the seashore and sit on a beach, or climb the mountain you have always wanted to climb. Rest.

Seven Soul Sisters began their journey on Summer Solstice, 2014

Womanhood. Behold in the Cosmos, Saturn actually determines when your adulthood beckons. Even though you have been bleeding for many Moons, this is the threshold where you embrace your full adult self. With this embrace, have you reclaimed some Soul parts? Where has your shadow appeared? What's in store during this arc of your life? Have you sent your heart out to locate your gifts? Often women dive into birthing the next generation, was that your path? I must ask again, who were you born to be?

Deepening Womanhood. This is the very middle of your life. Soon you can literally see Death traveling along as people you love begin to pass from this earthly dimension. You may consider yourself fortunate if your parents live long lives. My own parents crossed when I was 50 and 51. Then I became a baby Elder, alone and parentless. As a late bloomer, this is when my true life path began to reveal itself.

Elder Encore. You may live to be 100; this life-span elongation is the gift of our generation. This deep work remembering and reclaiming prepares you for that longevity. Now we've entered my territory, I am just learning what it feels like to be a Grandmother of the culture. In so many directions, inward and outward, you know all you need to create meaningful projects or connections, however you choose. More on this as your fully mature adult self looks to your Elder Encore.

Spiritual Elder. You have now re-examined your active life. Your intuition, connected to the Divine offers something as your legacy, what? Helping the younger generation review and heal their lives, this is ample work, more than we can do. Do you see your patterns? How can your life be of service to others before you pass? Are you preparing for that eventuality, Death?

Death. Nine Passages is complete with this final fiery, watery, earthy transformation. Your Soul becomes air, you are so well loved on Earth, you are greatly missed. Consider the Nature of your beliefs about Death and decide now if there is something you still need to do before your final Thirteen Moons.

This teaching comes from Angeles Arrien, The Power of Nature:[4]

Many indigenous cultures and spiritual traditions recognize four natural sanctuaries where we can remember and come home to who we are: the desert, the mountains, the waters and the woods. Nature comes from the Latin natus, "to be born." Native peoples look to these places for remembrance, Soul retrieval work, and to be reborn or renewed. Because we are made from the natural elements -- fire (our energy), air (our breath), water (our blood), and earth (our bones) -- we are always drawn to come into harmony with the beauty of Nature around us. It nourishes the Soul and opens us to be born into the mysterious presence and promptings of our own vast inner world.

**Hold in your heart the Four Directions,
the Four Winds, and the Four Colors of human beings.
Find a sacred breath in you for this trio of fours and begin.**

FOUR RITUALS TO MAKE YOUR OWN

**Moon Calendar
Writing Pages
Relationships and Events
Your Spiritual Bundle**

I would not ask you to follow rules, but as I guide you along this path I will offer suggestions. Two of my suggestions are great and important. I have already recommended that one or two [or more] friends commit to this journey with you. Your sisterhood may be linked in numerous ways. This pilgrimage will be an unforgettable journey to take together.

This second suggestion is just as wonderful: Each woman going on this pilgrimage needs to adopt, persuade, or trade with an Elder friend. Ask this friend to hold an energy space for your work, to be your Mentor, your wise advisor, and your witness. Please do this, trust me, she will be worth her weight in gold and silver. She will be a subliminal traveler and may do enough clearing and remembering work for her own Elder initiation.

From the beginning to the end of this pilgrimage, all of you will be inside of liminal time. Liminal time is a phrase borrowed from the Alaska natives; it means the shimmering time after you cross the first threshold until you cross back and return. In Rites of

Passage traditions, thresholds are crossed for the symbolic power of separating then from now; this separation will be more mental-emotional than physical. Life before this pilgrimage and life after are separated by liminal time and all that you don't know yet.

Your beautiful friend holding sacred space for you will also share this liminal time. So we can be clear, I will call her simply your Mentor. Somewhat aloof from your pilgrimage, she will be able to hold the lightening discoveries that you choose to share. She will listen when you need to share those electric discoveries and she will listen when you need to share your pain. Take time to talk with her about this whole process. Give her a copy of this guide. She will attend as you invite and certainly will earn her shawl when you complete your journey.

As you move through your natural history, imagine your four rituals. You can add more than I suggest. To step into remembering, the four rituals listed below will become a practice. You certainly will do your ordinary days as usual, e.g., work, entrepreneur, grandmothering, graduate school, family, all that you are up to right now. Also, you might be moved to apprentice with someone, attend a dream workshop, perhaps a dance class, or go on a vision quest before you complete your commitment and close the portal with your friends. You might do visioning with your circle or accept the challenge to go on a solo adventure while they create a safe backdrop for you.

Take time to breathe in the deep stillness of your inner world. As you breathe, use the stages of your development to help you reimagine the stories of your life experienced in earlier times.

Do your ordinary day like a multi-tasker. Your spirit, the very breath of you, shares O2 and CO2, oxygen and carbon dioxide, with every living thing. Nature will help raise your awareness, and activate your memory, even parts you thought long lost.

ONE

Moon Calendar. Since our lives are guided by the little squares on a linear calendar, I invite you to round those squares for a more feminine view, a round view of life. Use a calendar that shows New, Full, and Half Moons; during each of these Moon days make and keep a date with your busy self to go for a walk in Nature. By including this Nature walk on each of the Moon's exaltations, you join the heartbeat of our planet, New-Half-Full-Half. Don't you just love the beat? New-Half-Full-Half. Notice how the rhythm is circular rather than linear; thirteen moons make a year.

These long, quiet walks in Nature with the Moon will be instructive for you as a woman to deepen your understanding of the rhythms inherent in our natural world. These are Medicine Walks. Use them to sift through the a-ha's of your week, to deepen the time you are now reviewing; be open to receiving omens that will guide you through the next week. Watch the Moon and learn more about your personal rhythm. Expect your Moonpause or your Moontimes to settle into a rhythm with the Moon, a rhythm that belongs to just you. By planning carefully, your calendar will guide you. Invite the Moon to become a stronger ally. With your group of initiates, note the astrological Sun signs. Your rhythm will soon align with the Moon and the Sun. To move in the rhythm of the Cosmos, you begin when the Sun moves into a new astrological sign. Each review of a new life stage will begin this way.

If you are unfamiliar, learn about the design within these ancient patterns. Three signs make a season. Each astrological sign brings to your personal ecology a unique variation on the gift of the elements, earth, air, fire, and water. Your great ally in the sky, as constant as the Sun, the Moon moves in an ingenious way to raise your awareness as she follows the Sun.

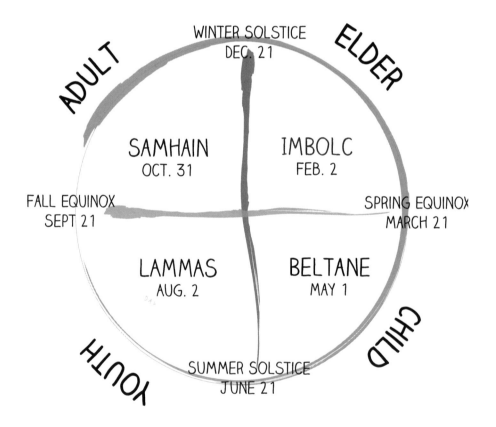

Women who hunger for spirituality find that it lives in plain sight. For a deeper connection to the Cosmos and the multiverse, open your spiritual self and look deeper. Discover how you feel about Astrology or any one of the other ancient oracles, the Tarot, I-Ching, or Runes. If you need to, challenge yourself to go deeper to transform those long held feelings. As I write the Sun is in Aries and many planets are aligning to create an interesting Grand Cross. I don't know why exactly, the more I pay attention, the more my fascination rises for all that is. The astrological calendar begins new each Spring Equinox. Six stages of your development can easily occupy six months and bring you across your first adult threshold. Decide now on the timing. How does one Sun sign for each stage feel to you? You are the weaver.

If you are a baby Elder, say 45 to 60, find the blessing in your Moonpause. You will be laying the foundation for the encore of your stages ahead. I use this term, encore, as the designation for Elders with more to choose and so much more to do. The current meme is 'your bucket-list.' If you are preparing for your Elder initiation, you already know that your rhythm offers low and high activity times. By observation, you will determine what belongs to you. Greater awareness is coming, catch yourself up for the children in your life. Choose well. One year will take you deep and heal many surprising aspects of your psyche.

TWO

Writing Pages. Begin a new journal and plan to write autobiographically every single day, on your schedule. In ten minutes, you can fill one whole page and lighten your mind while your spirit gets entertained. Spend ten timed minutes writing furiously about the current Passage in review; put your pencil down and close your eyes for a few moments to harvest from this memory immersion before you decide if you must write more.

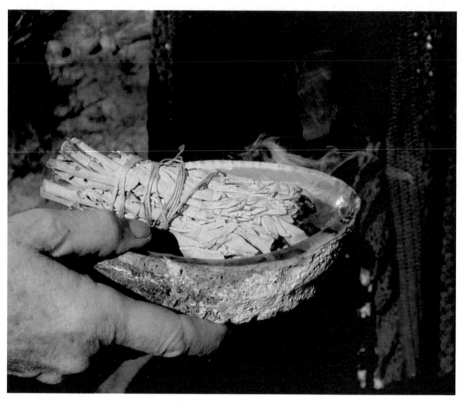

Ritual is prayer with an expression of love in your personal symbolic language.

I honor Julia Cameron[5] for giving us morning pages. Her design was produced for artists and writers. I have discovered that energetic writing on a timer, fully immersed, turns on something inside your engagement, pay attention. You will have written many pages in ten-minute increments with which to remember one life stage. You will see your choices and all the twists and turns that got you through that stage. Remembering deeply will call forth ordinary days and extraordinary events that funnel into your transition. This remembering, stage by stage, brings you back to yourself. This story of your life is folk psychology.

Just before the Sun again crosses into the next sign, a threshold of change will appear. In the alchemy of days, through remembering, journaling, and sharing, you will change. Before you step up to each threshold, prepare a quiet, heart ritual.

I have laid a stone spiral on the bank above the creek. For my Elder initiation, I moved a beaver-chewed log through the Life Spiral, one threshold at a time. I smudged myself there, my dog Rosie sat nearby, watching out, and I entered deeply into prayers of acknowledgment for my unseen spirit helpers and for all the gifts of my life, inner and outer. As I bent to touch a stone, I remembered a relation who had crossed my path in the past month. Like a crescendo, the power of this ritual practice increased through the seasons.

Through consecutive ages, you may remember things like an injury that sent your Soul out of your body. You need to retrieve and bundle any lost parts and breathe life back into them. You reclaim a little more of yourself as you work your way toward wholeness.

When you finish, when you feel quite done, you will have a written history of your life through the lens of inspired maturity. Looking inward will be easy and looking forward will be visionary. Please understand, this training realigns your brain and your neuro-pathways. The heart-mind core of you will take ownership and responsibility of your days in new and meaningful ways.

THREE

Relationships and Events. Often we are particular about who we call into relationship, other times our Soul does the inviting behind the scenes and we may only discover this wonderment through inner reflection. Relationships are how we grow and how our life experiences mirror back to us. Being human means finding our way through the internal, visceral reactions of our energy and belief systems. Abundant lessons, easy and hard lessons, are freely offered by others in relationship.

Along each segment in your Life Spiral, you met folks who moved on through soon after they gave you their gift; you also met friends who marked you with love. I invite you to notice how each relationship influenced you and altered your life's flow. In the stillness of liminal time and with your candle burning, I invite you to feel and be expressive with this remembrance. Art often satisfies your dramatic emotions whether you feel gratitude or something else. This remembrance offers insight for you and need not be shared. Express art for the people who loved you.

FOUR

Your Spiritual Bundle. Month by month, you will bundle your discoveries, those a-ha's and the parts and pieces of Soul Story that belong only to you. Art and dance can be allies to help you learn what belongs in your bundle. Your Soul-self came from Creator as a whole bundle, an energy bundle carrying gifts and primary instructions. Living in the modern world fractures this sense of wholeness. You may want to create a moving altar, an actual bundle that holds your sacred discoveries. Mine are safely held inside several journals, one each for child, adolescent, adult, where I combine art and word art.

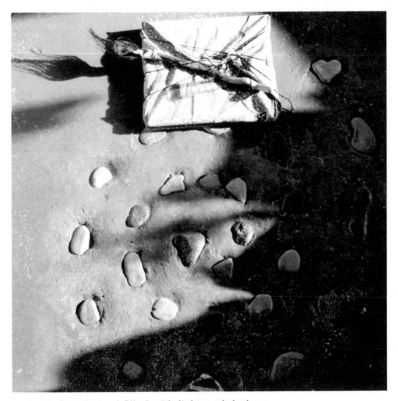

Author's first journal filled with light and dark

This pilgrimage through liminal time, observing how you were shaped is a Rites of Passage ordeal. To be true to form, you must accept a challenge, to move completely through the fire of transformation, you must test yourself. The purpose of combing through your memories appropriate to each successive age and stage will serve to return you to wholeness only if you do the work.

Bundling is gathering; I like both words. Create an intention to locate lost pieces of your Soul; discover what special gifts came with you at Birth; and go deeper with art, journaling, Moon walks, and your circle of confidants. Find time to look one another in the eye, learn to trust the truths of your voice: "I don't know what I think until I see what I say." These are the wise and enduring words of one of my blessed teachers, Clarissa Pinkola Estés.[15]

In the gorgeous movement of each day as you incorporate your many stirrings, you may discover your life had some kind of luck, but you may also have been turned by the hand of fate. Is this the hand of God? Did you encounter special moments sprinkled with fairy-dust? Before you cross each threshold and enter new territory, do your bundling of a-ha's to call that special energy back to you and heal your Soul.

Wisely use your journaling, wandering, and sharing. Place inside your bundle something to represent your discoveries, a reminder note, perhaps. Maybe your note will say Early Childhood on one side and on the other side, a phrase when you felt shame for the first time, or an instant when you felt lost and abandoned. Maybe you discovered your very own Shirley Temple talent of dancing and singing at age six. Write the notable memories of each Passage and place them in your bundle. Everything is important. I have enjoyed creating my bundle of memories; at each threshold, I carried them across to enter the next so that symbolically, I felt like I was creating a new bundle of myself, my Soul, and my gifts.

OTHER LUMINARIES

Enter Liminal Time and Space. With your mind in ritual, create a holy frame of mind, an altered state, a time and space apart that is yours and refreshed. Use anything you have that will invite and engage your Soul-self. Be inventive. To alter my mind, I begin with my altar. I know the two are related. My senses engage with the candlelight: sight, touch, smell, I ring a bell and dip a fingertip in Himalayan salt and touch my tongue. Once my body and my heart-mind are engaged, I invite my Soul to dance.

Passages require an 'away place,' a place where you can separate from your usual busy-ness to consider and create a threshold. Ritual is less prescribed than created.

Michael Meade, who demonstrates thrilling community rituals, says ritual builds in ascending order, from the ground up and begins with what you have nearby.[6]

Think of the words, rising, arising, connecting, reconnecting. You become Co-creator by inviting the Divine. Quiet music, flowers, incense, drums, rattles, lots of candles. In the woods, I leave the flame at home and use the dappled shade beneath a tree to reveal my light. After your commitment ritual with your Soul Sisters, invite a flow of ritual into your everyday, like swirling energy surrounding you.

You will begin to recognize that the seasons of your life have enriched your life as you reflect on this summer and that fall. Oh I do remember that winter! As they naturally occur and bring change, they may add an extra reason to celebrate. While you remember your childhood, for example, you begin to look inside the years and then the seasons within those years. What do you remember about summers before you went to school?

Equinoxes and Solstices dance with the Sun and offer an opportunity for ritual with a double meaning; they provide a reason for community and family celebrations and a frame for your pilgrimage. For all of my second married life, my playmate and I have stood before the Ancestors who hold the four directions and expressed our prayers of gratitude for the season just passing and the season ahead. For 20 years, I have loved a private celebration for the seasons' seasons, the first half and the second half. The second half of winter is marked by Imbolc, the second half of Spring by Beltane, the second half of Summer by Lammas and the second half of Autumn by All Souls' Day. Every six weeks, if we attend, the Earth presents us with a Holy Day for a ritual of simple and profound gratitude. [Refer back to page 36]

During this great expedition to the core of you, as you seek gifts or instructions you left unattended, grief will rise. That grief has been there all along. Allow, allow. You will also reclaim shadow and Soul parts cast aside; embrace and celebrate everything you learn. Put those special memories in a keeping place to receive some extra light and acceptance. Practice release, re-experience the small death of your former selves. Allow self-compassion to arise.

Those younger versions of you once were as real as anything that surrounds you today. Each one of your former selves still lives inside. The key to your wholeness lies in being able to embrace the earlier editions of you with all your exuberance, your great passion for ideas, and especially all your deep desires. Treasure these clues; they are the reason for this sacred Soul pilgrimage.

Commitment Ceremony. Think of what causes the world to pause or hush; that is ritual. What will give your experience extra depth and safe boundaries? That is ritual. You learn the essence of what ritual means to you through these answers.

Once you commit and your friends agree on the start date, please realize that your busy mind has engaged. From the very beginning of this journey—we have such busy-body minds—your ego fills right up with expectations. Each one of your expectations, even the buried ones, make the Creator laugh, but seriously each expectation needs to be examined. Write and talk about what you would like from this journey. What do you need? What do you expect? Wherever your family raises their eyebrows, gently offer salve. This pilgrimage has little to do with preconceived thinking; Divine discoveries will be delivered through this process of ritual remembering.

Your sense of ritual will grow as you encourage yourself to stretch into the quiet of your inner world. How you interact and if you are willing, your initiate friends will be as teachers for you. Your stillness practice invites your Soul to join you, to come back into your body, to reenter your dreamtime as well as your daydreams. Soul work is such a delightful discovery process. Help me bring this personal power word, Soul, back into our conversations.

Use Ritual. Even if you commit to spaciousness for this pilgrimage, as in separate and solitary, come together to design your plan. If you feel any angst, just light a candle and sit quietly. Fear comes up to be noticed and often while speaking, hearing you talk, fear will often return to the Earth. The candle and the quiet are two keys to unlock your own deep mysteries. Begin when the Sun enters a new astrological sign. Enter with a ritual designed by your group.

Once a month as the Sun moves, prepare a welcoming ritual for your next developmental phase. Decisions by the group will make this a solo or a group event. Decide about logistics and time constraints. Each threshold offers a bundling opportunity and demands that you honor the transformative fire of your thoughts with a ritual. Thresholds follow all through your transformative stages on the Life Spiral, which is complete at Death when you spin off to a new beginning.

As you stand before each threshold, give thanks to all those people and your Soul for placing you in time and space. Immerse your heart-mind in the earlier days of your life and step into the cloud of memories as if inside a bubble. Step across each threshold—drum, chant, and rattle with candles lit or fire in your belly. Betwixt and between[4] each threshold, you do life as you do, with an added dimension. The spirit of your body-mind and your dream-time floats in the bubble of remembering your life events of that stage and those ages, seeking new meaning and lost parts.

Once you commit to search for your Soul's instructions, that energy infuses your aura. Your life will do its own roller-coaster thing, as usual perhaps, but enjoy this new quality. The Universe will begin to cooperate. You may discover there is an energy that wants to dance, to trance dance, or to create heart projects with art and craft. Devote yourself to a daily creation practice to open you, even if your time is limited to 10 timed writing minutes and self-talk while you do chores. Perhaps some special expression will emerge each week. Remain vigilant in this search for your Soul instructions and reclaim any key passion you may have denied yourself. This may be just the opportunity to look at busy-ness. Discover or invent elongated moments for extreme self-care. Art and expression will carry you through any ups and downs like you're floating in a dream. Hang on for the ride of your life.

My Expectations. I am not shy in saying this path worked for me. Although I do have aging body challenges, I feel so alive after I finish writing about one major bundle of a-ha's. My fractured Soul parts have been gathered and my smile is perpetual. I have bundled all of my early years and dwell in astonishment that these

Passages revealed my Soul's original agreement. The early years hold my primary instructions. Before I feel truly complete, I will have done much digging and honored every one of my thresholds. I did cross my Elder Threshold on February 18, 2015, so you can locate my journey on a square calendar spot.

For you I expect this pilgrimage, this expedition, will culminate in transformative change and you very well may remember your Soul's primary instructions. You are going in search of your Soul's seeds, like bread crumbs left behind on your spirit trail. I will be honest to say locating your Soul's original agreement is the intention of this journey; to succeed will cause delight and celebration for all the years ahead.

BEGIN WITH CARE

Good. You have settled on a design and have agreed about when and how to start. This brings me great joy; I feel the same pins and needles you feel. Every Soul comes to Earth with a plan to learn lessons. Your primary instructions include your gifts which flow together to express your Genius. This pilgrimage to focus on your story will highlight Soul moments to piece together the bigger story.

Your great a-ha moments will create a matrix, in turn revealing the reason for taking this journey. When my great friend and original spirit sister said, "All the answers are inside you," she was not kidding.

A spiritual aura of sacred intent will surround you as you move through your days. As breath, your very spirit awakens in your lungs searching for your Soul-self. Your lungs awaken your whole body connecting you to the world around you. This connection is indigenous; everything exchanges air, CO_2 travels from our lungs to the plant kingdom and they give us O_2: plants and animals, we are all related.

Surround your spiritual aura with an air of forgiveness. I ask that you use forgiveness on judgments about your life. We come from pure intention to discover your Soul-gifts for wholeness. A ritual life leads to maturity and to evolution. That's the Elder's reward. I offer forgiveness to you for any moments you feel less enthused, less willing, less ready to take action to heal and move yourself into the higher realm of Soul and Genius.

All the moments of quiet, in Nature or in the presence of your candle, will begin to reweave your life. Women are weavers together. I will weave with you, you will weave with me, and for the Souls of the world's women, we weave a very strong plait with big-hearted intention. Throughout this time with Divine's sacred space, you may ask your Ancestors to be your witnesses. This journey of spirit is your own design; you simply borrow my design to hold you upright.

Bring to mind your Ancestors. Some of them you actually knew. Imagine an extensive line of Grandmothers and Grandfathers in your lineage; invite yourself back to their fire circles. Their lives were slower and less cluttered than yours. Visualize their culture and see the great differences. Imagine much farther back into your lineage, five or even ten millennia. If you can intuit their rituals, how they celebrated life and one another, then that thread of your own Ancestors lying in the dust can be recovered through this pilgrimage. This thread belongs to you and to us, to many Passage rituals coming back to the culture. The Rites of Passage thread will cause your Soul to tremble in celebration of life through these rituals of belonging.

If you send me a photo, I will put you on my altar.

Womb to Birth Threshold

Begin here in the Soul place before your Birth. Focus on your story of origin, your Soul story. Consider the time in history and your ancestry; meditate on this view and access your reason for being. Why did your Soul come to Earth when it did? For you as the initiate, this liminal time connects your spirit trail back through your lineage. As your own storyteller, you will gain a spiritual understanding of how the past shapes the present and the future. Remembering these pieces of your Soul story now fulfills a longing of your whole life. Everyone begins inside our Mother's womb. Design a ceremony using the same ritual elements your Ancestors used—fire, water, earth, and air. Sit as quietly as possible for a few moments and go inside with your thoughts and feelings. On Earth where gravity rules, all we know is time. This pilgrimage will help you identify gifts that came in with your Soul.

May I suggest something otherworldly? Use your imagination to enter the womb, float around at the end of an umbilical cord in the liquid bubble of the womb. Imagine floating with the Womb of the Universe. I actually mean to return your imagination to your Mother's womb. Claim a rebirth platform to remember your Soul story. Create an exalted connection with the storyline running when your conception was announced. What story did your parents create just before you came to be? How did neonatal care prepare for your Birth? You were needed and expected here on Earth. Soon you will know why.

Call forth your imagination; enter your wee oceanic body in your Mother's womb. You spent eight or nine months in the ocean of your Mother's womb, so spend time this month to call forth the intentions and instructions of your Soul.

Go inside this warm and spacious ocean preceding your first threshold. Begin to know yourself as the sperm meets the egg. Somehow you became the intersection of your Father and your Mother. Consider what gifts came through the environment of living with these two people. Other gifts came to you from this womb journey, gifts that were yours alone, gifts of your Soul. At some point your mind-body-spirit met your Soul, perhaps at Birth, perhaps before. This womb-time directs your Soul's journey.

Spend some time here and decide for yourself, what do you believe? How are Birth and Death related? Engage your heart-mind, dance like you were in the womb. Play ocean music. Every visual image you receive during this first month will ease all the rest of your journey. I advise releasing your right brain to the fine act of creating art!

Take time to breathe lots of air, very slowly. Use this time to learn how to quiet all the way down. Take long, warm baths, return to the womb in your mind. Review your developing body. Find the place of gratitude for your toenails, for your pancreas and liver and spleen, do some visual work for the miracle of your blood. While you are inside your Momma's womb, imagine her as an egg inside of your Grandmother's womb. That, in fact, is where we all begin. Remember this is no exaggeration, every one of your Mother's eggs, 400 or so, came through your Grandmother's womb first. We are miracles inside of miracles inside of miracles and need quiet time to honor ourselves.

Questions for your quest. To inspire your timed writing and help return your focus to this Divine mystery, listen to what Coyote asks: What story was already running outside the womb-space where you were born? While you did acrobatics at the end of your umbilical cord, what was the mood? What were the circumstances in your family of origin? What story do you know? Before you were born, did you come with an agreement about this lifetime on Earth? This womb-time spent in review is a perfect opportunity to challenge yourself to discover what you believe. Do your beliefs mirror your parents'? How did you form your beliefs? Did you agree to be here for a certain number of years and learn certain lessons? What state-of-the-world story can you piece together while you were inside that warm, wet womb space? When you were born was there any agreement about when or how you would die? See how many perspectives you can entertain.

It's important that you know what you believe for your origin story; Birth and Death have a relationship. Death walks with us through life and must be welcomed as a Soul choice, like Birth. Allow your cosmic consciousness to awaken to these questions. If you are open and curious, your beliefs will be revealed. Ask your own questions and share a sketch of your beliefs with your sacred circle. Can you speak your origin story to your Soul Sisters? I experience joy and humility when I consider my origin story. What do you experience?

The whole design of our human experience is free will. Why would your Soul choose your Mother? Why did your Mother choose your Father to be her mate? How did all of that happen anyway, what chemicals were racing freely through the world? Testosterone, estradiol, what part do you understand? We are truly much more than miracles.

I want to introduce Soul as energy of the Divine, the Source energy. While you are still in your womb-space consider the concept of your Soul as the bringer of gifts from the Source, does this fit in your belief system? Take this opportunity to understand how Soul fits into your personal cosmology. If terms like past life, rebirth, life after life, or life between life, offer clues, solidify these beliefs also. When you step up to the Birth threshold, you will know what you see coming.

Starting in the womb-space before Birth provides time and opportunity to preview the agreements between your parents as they cradled you. How did they prepare to receive your gifts and hold them safe for you? Parents are only one of our Soul's agreement; some of us have siblings who have been the closest confidants because of common origins. From the Cosmos your Soul agreed to also walk with your biological body and bring your cosmic mind into consciousness. Your cosmic consciousness wraps around mind-body-spirit at the peak moment of your Birth and then all that stardust seems to fold in on itself. Ask your sparkly cosmic consciousness to open beyond a rose bud to reveal more beautiful petals.

Consider why Soul is less talked about than other earthly experiences of human beings; we rarely share intimate meditations. If you begin a meditation practice just for this pilgrimage to review your life, more will be revealed and you will have an interesting perspective to share. Perhaps you could agree to an email drop to your circle of Soul Sisters and Mentors. Sharing your immersion will likely expand the vistas for every witness.

This time may be approached from many angles, try asking, what needs healing? Did you choose this warm and welcoming environment? Can you tell the story of why you made the choice of parents, of geography, and so many other details? What essential part of yourself came from your Father and what came from your Mother? For tender-hearts from divorced families, do you see and feel the difference between nurture and Nature? How can this reflective point of view expand your healing?

On the national and global historical timeline surrounding your Birth, what happened? Be curious. Wikipedia will help answer this curiosity for your origin story. Go there and plug in a date, like your birth year or conception year.* Your intuition is the best guide for this approach to review for healing. Remember you came with a purpose. Listening to your intuitive mind that delivers messages in subtle and complex ways will connect you to Source. Perhaps your purpose is already fulfilled or perhaps this pilgrimage will reveal the reason long known to your Soul-self. Look around to your friends now, how were their lives affected by history's timeline?

The emotions stirred by questions, mine and those you ask yourself, become clues to follow and journal about because the origin of your joy or pain lies somewhere in those emotions, not necessarily in plain view. While you have your mind in the womb-space, your biological creation brings a renewed appreciation for your body as a remarkable miracle. It brings into stark focus the need to think about your Soul.

* World population on the year of my Birth: 2,518,630,000.

If I asked you to please write a sweet letter to your Mother, do you jump at the chance or cringe? Nearly everyone has some kind of mommy-wound. Your personal experience may be well reasoned and understood or the consideration begins here while you're in reflection with her bulbous womb that became you. Your thoughts and feelings may fly back to this neonatal or postnatal birth time. Somehow mommy didn't attend quite perfectly. My Mother didn't nurse me, so at some point I decided she didn't love me enough. Here and now is where forgiveness rises in me and flows out.

Each one of us has our own definition of perfection for Mother. Without her perfect attention, we decide our Mother has abandoned us. This dance of attention and abandonment is reinforced each time you felt alone or did not have your needs met, perfectly. This rock and a hard spot is an old story for Mothers without many Aunties around. I let Mothers off the hook for this unfortunate cultural wounding wheel this way, as daughters we must realize we cannot know all the facts.

Write, dance, share and share more to heal those wounds for this reason if for no other: Culture has been far too hard on women; we bear so much unnecessary stress. This guilt and shame can be healed here and wherever it surfaces again. In Endnotes you will find Brené Brown,[7] an authority on the topic of shame and vulner-ability, how to recognize it, and what to do about it.

Perhaps it all started when Mother divided her focus while you were still an infant. Half of her attention went somewhere away from you and you couldn't get it back. This wounding is natural, we all have it because we made mommy our only focus. She focused on baby for much of your deep dependence and then returned to herself. This is true for more than half of all mommy-wounds. What were your specific details?

Before your Birth threshold, while in the wet and warm womb space, you will be opened by my suggestions. Take what is useful and leave the rest. Please get comfortable with your rou-tine as you flex and stretch to accommodate your new ritual hab-its. Write about everything in your heart and mind, write about your Ancestors who beckoned you to return to a body to complete your lessons. Then write about your parents, your siblings, and your earthly grandparents. Perhaps you hovered over the scene with your spirit guide. Once or twice each month, strengthen your circle with a call or a meeting. Your Soul circle needs you and you need them. Be willing to examine your inner realm, to heal and grow. Be willing to listen to your intuition as the Divine Feminine, the Source, or perhaps the voice of God of your understanding.

How you do what you do deepens this experience your way and leads straight to the drumroll—the Birth Passage which marked your emergence into the Earth plane and the whole of your life. The first and most dramatic of all of the Passages happens when your Soul meets your body.

The Ancestors wait for the moment of Birth, when the Masculine and the Feminine meet the Soul.

Birth Threshold

When you stand in your womanly body to cross this threshold of your Birth, declare your intention. If it is the precious vision of your whole life you want, say so. In this sacred place, everyone is listening. Your Ancestors—the long line of Grandmothers over your left shoulder, the long line of Grandfathers over your right shoulder—everyone is watching and listening, all of your Spirit and Animal guides, especially the Divine Masculine and the Divine Feminine. I call these combined energies many names and always mean the One Great Mystery and the Womb of the Universe, the Creator, God, the Source, or simply the Divine.

You emerged from the ocean of your Mother's womb. In a single moment your biology merged with your Soul, we all have had this one moment. Whoosh! Birth happens. Now, now! Step over your threshold. You came into this world on your own terms, with your unique astrological chart, unique finger, sole, and iris prints. Everything about you is unique including the gifts you bring as your offering to the world. Although you were born with a perfect forgetter, slowly releasing your original instructions back into stardust, this pilgrimage will recover those gifts and purposes brought by your Soul. The clues are yours to reclaim.

The spiritual journey of Mother birthing Child brings intense change for both. Religious icons may spring to mind. Be with the very second when air first entered your lungs and bow to that moment. This long anticipated Birth Passage is often well-attended. Your Soul has always had a journey distinct from your origin family so you and your Soul may need to get reacquainted.

Life begins with deep quiet, playfully watching the world. That is all we can do as new infants. Your baby self begins to test senses, eyes, nose, touch. Yum-m-m, Momma's milk. Watch everything. Look for Soul clues: Crumbs left lying around, this is what you will gather and reclaim.

Like the oceanic womb environment, remembering wraps you in a bubble filled with protection, with warmth and love, and with family dynamics. Birth brought you from the stars into your family of origin. In this quiet reflective time, rediscover your family traditions and dysfunctions. You knew them at a very young age but perhaps couldn't verbalize them.

These are anticipated moments, all that everyone could hope for, and the great awakening that follows becomes even more marvelous. Can you expand on the story at play when you began to breathe the air of your swaddling time as a babe-in-arms? At your moment of presentment with more thresholds before you, this might be an opportunity to take a shamanic journey with drums and invite your Soul to reveal herself. Perhaps a practitioner will guide the drumming. Perhaps you do this for one another. You are the ritual maker. Begin your joyful remembering by joining with your wee infant self, just after Birth, encourage your own remembering.

Ask for what you want and need to know about your birth story. If you feel like sharing, let your family know about your pilgrimage to revisit these Passage thresholds. Some of those family members have been part of your journey since conception. This will be good information as they may be the very ones to reflect your changes when you finish this pilgrimage. Perhaps your family would like to attend the closing ceremony of your transformation. Since this is a quiet journey, emphasis on quiet, perhaps the raucous party at the end is melodramatic. Change is often just quietly miraculous. What do you need and want from your family?

Early Childhood. In this liminal space between Birth and your childhood days, a story forms around your emergence and how well your Soul bonded with your body. See yourself. You are this one who wiggled fingers and toes first, then crawled at 6 or 8 months. All too soon, you lifted yourself up to sitting, then walking, talking, running, climbing. Your little child moved through a truly magical time of life. Rediscover the story of your training ground for life known as Early Childhood.

Time moved slowly between the Birth day, then weeks and months were counted and finally, your first birthday. This is life and death time for babies world-wide, but you fared well. How did you survive, have you wondered? What stories and fairie-tales helped you through? Can you still sing your favorite lullaby? Use your gift of imagination and connect to the Source. Tell your story with enthusiasm.

Birth begins your journey of 3000 days of childhood: Some days are well remembered. One friend recently told me that being pre-verbal and crib-bound, he looked up at Mommy and Daddy and very clearly remembers the scene and having the thought of looking forward to one day being able to speak to these parents. Every cobblestone between Birth and Middle Childhood on the Life Spiral holds your dramas of Early Childhood in its entirety. Much is beyond remembering.

Allow your imagination to fill in your memory, photos help a great deal. So much change happens even before you turn five; with this immersion, you might be surprised what bubbles up. Be surprised: Holding space for stories causes them to appear out of the ether, like magic. You are looking for clues to all the things you loved, your gifts, and wounds that need to be healed, the places where you left pieces of Soul-self behind. We all have some memories missing; such is the nature of remembering and forgetting. Place your focus on the surroundings, your siblings and friends, any considerable trauma or injury, and borrow this saying, "More will be revealed." The more you look, the more you will see.

For your writing pages, consider how to revisit every one of your days. Hold these questions tenderly—What did you come to do? What gifts did you bring? What are you supposed to do with your life? Early Childhood was your training ground for life, do the family traditions still hold their meaning? When you realized dysfunctions were operating, how did you play along? What was good and bad? From this perspective, you may enjoy the observation over any judgments. As a baby and toddler, you were hardly prepared for self-care, not yet. Did you receive good care, some care, Grandmother care, neighborly care?

In your writing pages, entertain musings about the people who adored you and who touched you in some way—a heartfelt way, an intrusive way. Many people influenced your first 3000 days. Who made up your village? Have you ever truly wondered about human development and how slowly ontogeny—the biology of growing into adulthood—happens? What stories helped you through? How many band-aids did you need? Maybe you still need to lift a few of those and heal what was hurt.

From Janis: "I am creating a list of all those who touched my early childhood, and what I remember about them. Did they love me, were they kind, funny?"

As you grow, you will need to wrap this bundle of feelings, of stories, images and gifts. For the next few days you will feel the wave washing over you. Only days before, in imagination, you stood on top of this oceanic wave, now you dive deep within the trough, within yourself.

Most often, we forget the primary instructions that accompany our Soul born to this Earth world. I believe that forgetting your primary instructions happened slowly, slower than we can imagine. Children still see fairies if they are lucky, until someone hushes their sharing. Little children, natural Divine beings, are much closer to the Creator than coddling adults. Ask your wee self to tell you all you need to know. Ask the messages to come; a month will be spent here in this wonderland of growth and change called Early Childhood.

After Birth, you bonded to someone, who was it for you? That bond is crucial, your destiny and lessons depend on understanding your first bond. In a mysterious psychic dance, events formed that foundational relationship and now offer keys to your own psyche and your Soul as an adult. By the time we begin to consider needs and wants with our logical mind, we are already 8 or 9 years old. By then, this original bond has penetrated our psyches with thousands of hooks. Most of them are good-for-us hooks like personal safety and hygiene. Manners and kindness gel early. Did you become an ice cube, frozen into a certain shape? It seems so sometimes. This is why your wild Soul emerges and discovers the thrill of feeling unruly, rowdy, dirty, and earthy. That's logical, everyone has this earthiness inside.

Do at least one, special blank-page art project for this Birth through little child time: Begin blank and big, maybe 11x17 or bigger. Use whatever medium or tools, collage or not, to create a lost and found piece, colorful, symbolic, of your experience of dredging, remembering, honoring, releasing. This begins your life history portfolio. It's perfectly good to write circularly around the edges— well, there are no rules and you may be limited mostly by time. Take time for this, as long as you can spare yourself. By engaging your right brain, art for joy and without judgment, will coalesce your Soul pieces, nudging them back to wholeness. What happens next?

Light candles while you are working, especially if you remembered trauma of being a child. To evolve your Soul, linger on the time when you were an exuberant personality, 2 or 3 years old. The world may have already said no and don't a few dozen times by then. How did those words cut your animation? This is where your Soul-slicing experiences within nurture and culture need to be searched through to recover and remember your enthusiasm for wholeness. One last time, visit the seasons of your young child's life and do art to heal yourself.

Please, little child, before the Sun changes its sign and before you stand on the threshold as a Middle Child, half grown, please plump out your journal with entries about childhood. Identify your wounds from Early Childhood, before age eight and write them on a list. Fold your wound list into a tiny bundle and wrap it with cloth and string. You have just begun a practice of bundling your discoveries. Take the list to your Mentor, your taproot and ask her to hear your stories. Ask her to reflect any and all gifts that she sees from these openings in your Soul. Wounds and gifts are separated by only a membrane. You will do this a few more times so the symbol of Early Childhood needs to be small but not invisible, carried over the next threshold and then safely set aside.

Art like story and movement offers true and lasting healing.[8] To add a release aspect to your art project, you could even draw the pain and burn it in a ritual fire. Wrapping the bundle of this time is like making a shroud for your child self. One facet of ritual initiation, which allows you to move into the next stage of your development, is the little Death of the self you're walking away from, this requires clarity and intention.

You now have a rhythm with daily ritual and find slowing down a practice to hear your Soul-self. Do you engage with an oracle, wisdom cards, animal medicine, Tarot, Astrology, trance dance, Reiki? Self-care exploration offers so many options. Do you take long baths or tune in for a message in other ways?

You are on a life-changing pilgrimage. Be aware of your inner desires. Your ally, the Moon moves from New to Full and back again always ready to help celebrate your exalted time through her crescendo. On your Moon walks, please take a stroll through your fairie-like memories of being little and look for signs of your child-self in Nature. What animal walks with you? Did you imprint with an Aspen tree when you were a babe? In the midst of ceremony, one of my Elder teachers remembered her imprinting with Aspen leaves and I have never forgotten her story. Her cloth cradle swung beneath the quaking leaves of an Aspen and she became imprinted with the quaking leaves. While she told of how it felt, we all watched her fondle an Aspen leaf and that imprinting transferred to her listeners.

In these next few days, allow a little breathable air to move around before the next threshold appears. Be sure time is spent to write down those gifts and a-ha's before you make this move.

Celebrate Middle Childhood

Middle Child Threshold

Hopefully you have spent just the right amount of time with your child self. If this is true and you feel the age of responsibility pushing you up to the next threshold, then, drumroll, create a ritual that will welcome this fresh-faced, innocent big girl into her next stage of development.

Bend a willow stick and make this girl a crown of flowers, dress her up in her finest, beloved dress. Brush the wild knots out of her hair and give her a bit of a smudge with sage. Allow ritual to enter and swirl around your mind to make a new threshold plan. Do a ceremony to reset your liminal sacred space with no distractions, alone or not. This Middle Child Threshold may be a line in the sand or a row of flowers; it may be a root or your rattle. Lay something in front of you and close your eyes. Renew your commitment to spend enough time exploring with your girl-self. She was you who fanta-sized with fairies and built them secret houses in the tall grass. This girl will teach you everything about your Soul-self. Listen carefully to all she wants you to remember. As she casts about, she begins to claim her gifts. Respect your big-girl self and allow her back into your memories, welcome your true self back into your heart. Be certain you feel ready to move. Be on time with this ritual and make a little ceremony or a big ceremony.

This ritual Passage known as Middle Child is the ceremony that invites more as the mental doorway to consciousness opens for all the other Passages. This one sets the tone for the rituals that will grow you into your full woman's bloom. At this portal, your baby self is no more. Stand tall to face the glory years ahead and invite your memories to open and illuminate your big girl self. Your girl within is waiting to spend this time with you and discover what needs to be wrapped in her bundle. She wants you to weave a ritual that you will not soon forget. Tell your initiate sisters your child-hood story and why you feel more grown up at 8 or 9 years old.

Can you see her? Ah, here she comes, you as a Middle Child. Pull out your third and fourth grade pictures. Spend some time with her and she will remind you about the profound sense of self that came in with these years. I feel so much tenderness.

Middle Childhood may be the very place to find your prima-ry instructions. Emily Hancock[9] interviewed women over 70 and heard them say this time, the *girl within* was a peak time of their lives, the most of everything, the most magic, the most fun, the most daring, the most mysterious, and the most free.

You may discover a matrix of clues about yourself, no lon-ger little, not even wanting to be bigger. Give her enough of your tender loving attention and she will reveal herself as the keeper of your original identity. Emily Hancock called the time spent as a big girl "the real fertilization of the female" and strongly advised such a review may bring you "back to the girl she is in the first place." Remember your story from this time. A true healing will be yours if you honor yourself through art and movement.

This time is an especially potent time to watch the Moon every day. I say this thinking of the next thresholds ahead. Sweetly attending to the Moon will initiate you by aligning your biorhythms to her light and her energy. Sometimes your habits only need a thought, daily Moon watches, oracle readings, and journal writing. Is your calendar marked to remind you to take your solo walks with the Moon? Adopt specific suggestions that fit you—candles, altar making, meditation, quiet-dreamy wanderings, singing, dancing— these make a ritual life.

The Full Moon walk for this Sun sign will bring your exalted time to a crescendo. Please take another stroll through your fairie-like memories of being pre-pubescent. Remember that solo strolls under the Moon are known as Medicine Walks for a reason; just look for signs from Nature. Remember, remember, remember this deliciously alive big girl time, way before puberty, when your true self emerged. Repeat your commitment to spend enough time digging into your girl-self who climbed trees and stretched your parent's rules to suit yourself. What else is there? Who helped you? If you want more here, I helped celebrate 5 girls and wrote a long story for Middle Child Rites, as the first half of the girls' ceremonies on my website.[10]

As I was about to enter Middle Childhood, two of my closest friends moved away and horses became my new best friends. One week two odd accidents marked this threshold for me. I was riding a horse double with my older sister, but the ride was rough and boun-cy and I couldn't hang on. When I hit the ground I broke my arm. Always ready to get back on a horse, just two days later, I asked for a ride down the block to home. I fell off that tall horse and landed on my head in front of our neighbor's house. The state patrolman saw this accident and carried me home. I was unconscious for a while, how long I am not sure, but I spent a quiet week, broken arm and almost broken head, closely attended by my parents. This is my second clue that Rites of Passage is my Soul's purpose. Because I was four months away from my ninth birthday, I learned that Passages happen on a Soul schedule rather than a birthday schedule. Without proper attention to Soul, a threshold may appear in a crisis. I remember feeling grateful to be alive and I appreciated my young body so much. I remember that falling didn't make me afraid. I was always in peak happiness on horseback. Remembering back is the jewel—ceremony is ritual and ritual invokes quiet—my Soul had created that little accident as a gift for me to harvest.

Perhaps you remember your threshold from this time long ago. Story your time in your writing pages. Stay in the cosmic rhythm with the Sun, go deep into your memories at this liminal time to remember how it was to be a big girl. Bring yourself into alignment with the ritual rhythm you love and with your initiation companions.

Offering up juice for your journal time, I reach into mythology. Michael Meade said recently, "Our past is always present." An all new level of awakening began to open in me when I heard him tell the story of Poder[6] and then ask this question, "What great and potent gifts were you born with?" Can you name your gifts? Do you recall what was important to you in elementary school? Did you have more fun out of school? What mischief did you specialize in? What did you dream about?

In this story, Poder had an advantage over us moderns because at his Birth, the midwife took care of the gifts that came with him until he was old enough to take possession and learn how to use them. That is what this age of Middle Child is all about, claiming your gifts and learning how to master them. Does any of this ring a bell for you? What if you could now enter this Poder story at age 9 as you stepped up for more responsibility in your life? What if your gifts were simply brought to your attention and you started to coax them into form?

It is my strong belief that this threshold and liminal time is very special. Each Soul swirls and twirls while your expanding Earth loving mind awakens in Nature. Outside play may have caused a loud inner gong directing your life to unfurl with a Nature thread. Maybe your Soul sang a message from the territory of the Divine. At this Middle Child stage, your true wild-self emerges. So much of life opens during this time. I remind you about the purpose of this pilgrimage along your spirit trail: Right here, before puberty, your authentic self dreamed and she made plans. Some of those dreams and plans still wait for you to remember, to reclaim, or grieve. These years add juice to every year that lies ahead.

For your journal writing and immersion pages, what else is there? Who helped you? Can you imagine all the parent-friends who guided you? Did anyone actually mentor you? So many people crossed your path and gave you a small gift, can your big-girl self recall some of those? Your being is fresh, still quite little and inno-cent. You moved into and through the third to the sixth grades for your birthdays, 8, 9, 10, and 11. As your memory flashes, who were you? What did you like and dislike? Who were your friends? What made you swoon?

The Sun moves slowly giving you permission to move slowly. Are there any clues in Astrology for you? Was there an event or a birthday or a holiday that firmly anchors this time? Why do you think you remember some things so clearly? What did you want your life to be at this special between-time when you were more than a child and less than a teen? From your perspective as a big-girl, you face the glory years ahead, the early teens. Not yet pubescent, this is a good time to look to the stars and dream the dream of your life.

Sometimes life seems to be all about wounds to test how we go about healing them. Tell your Mentor when you locate wounds that need to be remembered. Maybe your wounds need to be burned in a flame to release their hook. Hopefully, your Mentor will remind you that wounds and gifts are but a shining membrane apart from each other, and they are related. Wherever you felt wounded, your gifts lie very near.

You've entered this training ground to daily watch the Moon, be thorough. Soon, the New Moon or Full Moon will invite another solo Medicine Walk. You definitely need your Soul Sisters at this time. Write like a mad woman to prepare and then gather and tell your big-girl story around a safe and sacred fire circle.

Soon though, the Middle Child grows ready and willing to dance her way to puberty and her First Blood ceremony. Proceed ever so slowly. The sacredness of that old story needs to be honored and revisited with ritual. If none of your Passages were ritualized, doing so in this way will heal the old and lay down a new story.

Think deeply about this age of responsibility as a sacred Passage. Your girl worked hard to lay the foundation for your woman-self, while she expressed every ounce of your Soul's message in actions, in daydreams, in passions. Often those messages flowed through you for just a single day. Some of the stronger messages from your Soul repeatedly drop bread crumbs for you to follow.

Spend enough time here to discover your Soul identity. How did your 11 year old self determine so much of your future? Beneath her were foundation stones provided by loving [and often stressed] parents. She feels positive, negative, yin and yang balanced. She feels capable and fragile. Her different mood swings signal a settling into her hormonal and normal biorhythms. Your mind may travel into the past at will but have you ever gone into your memories to search out Soul clues? The mind expansion that brings a girl to age 11 astonishes neuroscientists, almost as much as what's ahead when the adult brain fully transitions at age 14. At the ages of 11 and 12, the capacity to be child-like and adult-like as a chameleon surprises even you. How can you expand your consciousness? Have you delved into your oracles like Tarot and Astrology?

For many girls, their Grandmother Stories carry a potency needing to be remembered. This is especially true for big girls who have an imprint for life from one or both of their Grandmothers and Othermothers. What potency can you remember from the stories of these other women? What astonished you about how their lives differed from your parents?

In these next breathable few days, allow air to move around a little before the next threshold appears. Consider your five elements for ritual; I seem to always bring water. Consider the power of this big-girl's story you have received through searching. As you do art, fold your gifts, your Soul-slivers, or a-ha's received during this time into your bundle. Write furiously in your journal about what you learned about your young self. Be with yourself. Be.

If you're stuck, alter your mind with art, seek a zone of concentration different from your usual activity. You might rearrange your altar space and light a scent to bring about your ritual mind.

Even though I suggest a death ritual before you cross the next threshold, remember, it's only meant to sever your attention not to diminish your memory. Your past is always accessible, especially now that you've added stories about this time to your journal. You may find, as I did, that this is such an amazing time, you will need to linger or come back for a visit. Doesn't it feel fabulous and rare to enter these truth telling memories with and about your Soul? Like your child-self, this big-girl persona will go right across this next threshold with you and will always be available to call on, especially now that you have renewed your relationship.

Go ahead, call in a symbol for Death, perhaps a snake that readily sheds her skin. Welcome this teacher. Ask for closure on this time so that you might float across the next threshold. Express gratitude as you lay down and close your eyes. Pull the cover over your head and meditate to release this beautiful big-girl back into her innocence. Her Blood is coming.

First Blood Threshold

Through remembering, return your heart-mind to the threshold time when your blood first appeared. Blood is the catalyst for change and the only threshold so obvious no one argues about the timing. The days you share a cycle with the Moon are called Moontimes by women like me. A special characteristic of our Boomer generation is how our cycles were hidden from sight, hardly ever talked about. Quite a few of us never received one word of instruction, even when we complained. Do you still hold shame around your periods? We moved through the myriad of biological changes like every new young woman, from height, weight, pubic hair, armpit hair, acne, enlarging breasts, and finally First Blood. I feel grateful when I hear that any part of this much needed information came as a pure-heart offering from another woman who also bled. The old ways of telling you about blood and showing you a napkin, leaving you to tend, those ways and those days are dwindling away.

Resist, it's so much fun to be a girl! Surrender, the blood means you're going to be a woman. Resist-surrender, it's the dance every girl performs. Inside the persona of your new young woman you may feel a sigh of relief; finally there is a way through menses, through blood, a way that is glorious, sacred, and purposeful. I teach girls to sit in stillness looking back over the last month and looking forward to the next. The twin energies of review and intend provide building blocks for life. I call this visioning or women's vision quest. Reimagine your bleeding times as Moontimes and give yourself permission to step away from usual duties for a time to enjoy a women's vision quest. Lucky girls will now do this every single Moontime. Can you write a new story for yourself by closely watching the Moon?

There may still be a fairie princess inside of you, 12 years old about to turn 13, still pumping her legs to push her swing higher and higher. She doesn't want to grow up. For these *Soul Stories*, call forth your adult-self because she can manage. Invite your ceremonial-self to design a ritual with tempo and timing that swirls around and comes from your heart. Life is about to change dramatically.

The hormones that bring puberty to a big-girl's world may seem the cruelest trick of chemistry. Stand before this threshold and feel a tinge of sadness for your big-girl self. Before you bid her adieu, ask her to juice your dreamtime with the essence of your Soul being. Ask yourself, who were you born to be? You had a good time for those brief 1500 days of Middle Childhood, but Blood changes everything.

Be brave, step gently across your lovingly made threshold and feel tender for the darling of a girl suddenly visited by a woman's experience. Blood on your panties, it happened more than once to every single woman on the planet. Not too long ago, women felt shy, perhaps even ashamed to speak about this experience. Was that true for you? Go deeper into your memories. Suddenly this thing called puberty invites multiple personalities and voices like a critic and a judge to live inside your head.

Out of necessary deep compassion, remember your true story before you re-story. Did you live with those washed and stained panties? How many outfits did your blood stain before you found the Moon's rhythm with your body? Women, this includes you and me, we were so hushed with this conversation. Did you talk with your sisters at least? What did your womb feel like? We must remember this curse-n-rag story to bring about a completely different experience for our granddaughters and our great-grandaughters, too. I wrote story essays, with good ritual ideas for Middle Child Rites and for First Blood, and published them together into one Kindle formatted book called *Girls' Ceremonies of Nine Passages.*[10] For your time of renewal and visioning, now is the time for you to remember your own experience.

For many years I was gripped by a question offered up to women by Judith Duerk in her precious little book, *Circle of Stones.*[11] It is a thoughtful question, a grief filled question, a question with possibilities for change: "How might your life have been different if there had been a place for you, a place for you to go, to be with your mother, with your sisters and the aunts, with your grandmothers, and the great- and great-great-grandmothers, a place of women, a place of women to go, to be, to return to, as women? How might your life have been different?"

Whether you were shy or boisterous, something happened to your developing psyche every time you released the blood of your cycle. How can you pierce your own protective shell and remember this new young woman-self? In what way did you feel connected to God or the Source, to the Divine Feminine, and through your Soul to your psychic self? These are sensitive memories and you need to be tender with moments remembered as they arise. As yourself today tracks back to when you were a new young woman, spend time here to celebrate the Birth of your actively conscious being. Did you realize your psychic self and your Soul were your inner companions on this Earth journey? Visioning takes you to the territory where Soul dwells and still holds your gifts and your purpose.

There is little for you to do really, except become as quiet as possible and be your Soul's witness. You witnessed the vision of your life as it was revealed. Attend well to the grief that may rise and caution your inner judge to hush; this is your quiet remembering time. Interactions with parents reveal so much. Do you remember how they tried to hang on to your childhood? I wonder what generation of parents leaned on this poem for their spiritual support?

On Children by Kahlil Gibran:[12]

> Your children are not your children.
> They are the sons and daughters of Life's longing for itself.
> They come through you but not from you,
> And though they are with you yet they belong not to you.

Since you have storied through the age of responsibility and begin to grow now into your adult brain, you feel and act in charge of yourself; I invite you to do ritual your way. I am still holding firm to the edges of your dance space and remind you of the ritual elements. Those darn Coyote questions for your writing pages come fast and furious. You have kept dates with your Soul Sisters and you have walked with the exaltations of the Moon. This is such an important time of your life. Have you formed a clear picture of your personal ecology? Have you remembered your First Blood story? Who supported you during this time in your life?

How do you interact with the girl who slowly and awkwardly moved into your woman's body? Moontime is not the only story of puberty. What are the memory-marks of your early and middle teen years? Were these years hilarious or sad or both? Did you read? Did you sing and dance? Did you paint? Were your days marked by fantasy, science fiction, or wild dream collages? Spend some of your "now" moments to be with your teen self who loved to _____. Who were you and what did you love to love in each of the years, 13 and 14? What were your persistent preoccupations? Do you remember how you entered the world of women with hair, make-up, and dress?

I suggest an art project. You have entered the mind space as an early teen woman who simply cannot see how much change lies ahead. Make a plaster mask of your beautiful face; go online and get directions and materials. This mask comes in so handy at the next threshold. First get it made and then set it on a nail to dry. If you put this mask in a place where you can see it, soon the blankness of your young face, the blankness of your life will begin to haunt you. You were not a blank, but what did you feel, exactly? I would love to hear that your Soul Sisters made an afternoon out of this mask-making adventure. As teen girls, we did our best to avoid confrontations with adults, so ask your adult self to take a timeout so you can spend time with your teen self.

Find a little space of time to lie down and put on your mask and re-enter your dreams about who you were becoming. The mask helps your girl to enter an altered space, something young girls love to do. In this altered space, dreams come easily. What did you dream about when you were an early or middle teen? I am imagining from my own story and girls I am with now: Does daydreaming ring any truth about how you spent time with yourself during puberty?

Perhaps now a bit hazy, these days were your making-of-a-woman years. Exploring your feminine body and capacities is always important to teens. How did you honor your body through these explorations? Did you learn self-care? How did media and peer pressure influence how you felt about your body? Did you spend a lot of time in the bathroom, in front of a mirror, putting on makeup? How did girlfriends influence you? As a young teen, how did you view your body? How has your body image changed over the years? Can you unearth and heal any shame? Be sure to visit with your Mentor around body image.

Do you remember the emergence of your emotional self? I remember my early and middle teen years as wholly emotional, nothing else seemed to weigh in like my emotional state of being. Can you remember and tell yourself, in your journal, the whole truth about your teen years? Take those 10 minutes at a time, writing fast, bring your automatic writing to an altered state where truth and memory meet.

Do you remember how you negotiated being physically and emotionally connected [or not] while you held firmly to your values and boundaries? What qualities did you bring to your friendships? This question is applicable for girlfriends and for boyfriends. This is your pilgrimage, what questions do you need to ask your teen self? Did mean girls use you or were you a mean girl? How did you set boundaries with a partner? How did you negotiate that without driving someone away? How did you deal with the pressure to have sex?

Do you remember how it felt to be a daughter and a woman with your Mother? Did you talk about important things or avoid them? Did she try to communicate? Did you try to communicate? Many have tried, but the story of mothers and daughters has not really been told. Maybe for you and for your Mother, the story has just begun to be told. Maybe little snippets of your mother-daughter story is known to your family, but what was your whole story? I have three sisters and we have very different mother-daughter stories. These teen years were an especially crucial time for this relationship. Wounds not healed often last for decades. This is a rare and precious opportunity to name those stories, share them, grieve them, and heal them.

These are long years, the early teens, maybe even torturous, but now it seems they passed in a blink of your eye. How many years ago was that for you? As you review these years, be gentle with yourself; be gentle with your memory of your parents, siblings, and teachers, as well. After answering all my questions and your own, hopefully you will feel reconnected with your early teen years. This age can feel simultaneously free and glorious, somehow you find yourself awakened and interested. You may have felt frightened and doubtful. How did your young woman-self hold all those emotions at the same time?

You have the opportunity to put your training wheels back on and remember. The unique combination of a rapidly maturing brain and female hormones cause a bit of a whirl, but after a year or two a new normal emerges. You will learn to stand inside your story once again. But you don't know that yet. Your junior high years were another world. Use compassion as you visit with yourself at the tender ages of 13 and 14. All young people are in pain and at risk now. Was this true for you?

Do you remember what worked for you to form an identity that served you in making good choices? How did you challenge yourself? What did you want to master? I ask you to look deeply and to feel deeply. Where do you find lingering regrets? What did your Soul want from life, from you?

Meditate on this Circle of Courage shield.[13] In your imagination only, you are on the cusp of 13 and 14. What do you wish you had experienced at these tender young ages as a new young woman? How did you perceive belonging? If you felt generous during the holidays, were you generous the rest of the year? How you arrived at independence will be your memory challenge as your teen years roll through high school.

When I first remembered my teen years, I was studying human ecology and development. I often employ this Circle of Courage symbol when I share with young teens. I look ahead with them and imagine this shield as a challenge. Working through your adult self now, using truth and intent with reflection, can you see that something may have been missed during your teen years? This is true for all of us. Did you ignore some Soul knocking message? What was the message from your Soul that you longed for? These discoveries are the point of this pilgrimage.

Outward focus and good mentoring was all I needed when I was 15; instead, I folded in on myself and grew miserable with my small town life. I did play the piano well, I played it for emotional release and I played it to vent my endless frustration; there was nothing like Beethoven! How did you fare during your own middle teen years? Did you feel a bit lost or flustered? What was your release? Fifty years ago risks were different than today. I didn't know a risk until I left home and then risk became all that was simultaneously terrible and wonderful. How did you approach risk and when?

On this pilgrimage your purpose is to heal. Every event, birthday, and holiday needs to be opened, examined, and reassembled. This happens in the bubble of your thoughts and when you lay your head down. The purpose is to ask what clues, what gifts, what parts of yourself were left lying beside the trail that reflected your Soul's great destiny. Was it a relationship or a choice that caused you to become smaller?

We are first and always our most reliable source of information. What gifts did you know about but ignored during these precious years? Usually you know, the emergent hormones and emotions often filled you with passion for something besides sex and being a fashion statement. What made you feel overwhelmed with desire? Do you have a flawed or a flawless memory? What were you really good at? What were you most interested in? Did you take time to master a skill? What were your greatest moments of courage?

What did you learn from having your Blood come regularly? Did you understand anything about it? Did you know that for the next 40 years, minus pregnancies, you would bleed every month? I talk about Moontimes because I see the four to ten cycle days each month as opportunities. As a new young woman, somehow you settled into acceptance that each month you would bleed. Blood is power, it always has been. Revisit your experience and consider entering the deep quiet of rest with candles lit and music playing to rejuvenate your experience.

All women have a relationship with the Moon. If your connection with La Luna is either slack or lacking, you might want to increase your cosmic consciousness by tracking every day in the Moon's cycle for a few months. Simply add the Moon phase to your date-entry at the top of your journal. Find the Moon in the sky, watch her. She's not all that easy to track. This is generational connection, all of our Grandmothers were guided by La Luna. Designate each New or Full Moon as your very own to create vision boards, Soul collages, fabulous poetry, or original music.

As you review your teen experience you could take advantage of this time to treat yourself and get treated in a way of your choosing. You would have the support of several generations if you simply decided and told everyone how you would spend your Moontimes: Alone, with other girls, in ritual, doing art, listening to music, not attending school, not going to work. You have less trouble designing your time now, how things have changed!

When you were younger did you understand the sequence and purpose of your hormones? Your mental, emotional, physical, and chemical combinations helped to determine how they sequenced. Being in balance or not has the power to change your pattern over time. Remembering your Blood time, when your cycle was obvious, did you choose rest? Did you know that energy flows high to low to high again with the rhythm of your cycle? I knew nothing of this and found myself forcing energy during low energy times. In my life, there were decades of that behavior. Proper rest and time to vision and understand my life, that would have been infinitely more beneficial through the Blood days of each month. Did you give enough attention to self-care, good health, and relationships to develop nourishing habits?

Relationships with family and peers were developmental foundation stones. Pain does seem to leave its mark during this first half of adolescence. What were your low-lights? Did dwelling on these prevent high-lights from appearing? Remember you are excavating for Soul. Keep it personal and recall your relationship with each family member. Were there family activities that you truly loved? Were you bound or free? Did you dream only of the future or did you live in the present? Have any of your teen patterns persisted? Did you watch the clouds and daydream?

If you could pick out the highlights of your years before age

17 or 18, when you left home, can you fondly recall the windows of joy? Did you think your facets were polished? Could you feel excitement about leaving the nest? How did you ask for help with the final polishing? Did your girl-gang help one another do that?

I should tell you now: The first rule of managing in the adult world is you make it up as you go along. You may not have been able to get this true confession out of your Mother and Grandmother, but it's true. Women navigate this way; creating a home for ourselves, teaching our loved ones, entering the workforce, we create in the moment. We live in a world of active imagination.

Your imagination is activated by Nature. I consider it completely outrageous that this truth for living a whole and fulfilling life is often left behind in childhood: Sit quietly with Nature to awaken your imagination and your solutions will seem to come from nowhere and everywhere. You, too, can make it up as you go along. Our one luscious, chaotic, and generous Earth provides juice for visions. Frankly, I want your teen self to see this truth, she will reinforce capacity for your Elder self. Limitless as you have always been, consider deeply: How did it feel to be wildly creative and make a few things up on your own? Can you see the assist from the natural world? Did you need more women to bounce things off? I wish someone had told me about the secret of stillness.

Staying with this indulgence, I suggest the bonus to re-submersion in puberty is viewing the early creation of your Elder self. Here is where you received your first clues about how you would be as an old woman. If you can find ways to honor you teen self, you will also be honoring your future Elder self.

When you recognize and feel maturity, move your inner energy system, your chakras, into alignment with your purpose. This may cause fireworks, personal a-ha's. Good! Grand, actually! Journal and talk—this is what we would suggest our young friends and granddaughters do. Epiphanies need to be honored, solidified, and felt deeper in your body.

You will begin to recognize marks or lack of maturity in the ones you love.[14] Make the most compassionate note of those thoughts, but redirect all of your focus back to you. Take no action until your personal transformation is complete. You are the director of your own show. Since you were a bud of a young woman, you have been a culture maker. Trust that those who wait for you to complete this pilgramage have received their spiritual message to wait because your initiation will shine a golden light all through the younger generations.

To close out this first half of adolescence and fly free into the second half, dream up your First Flight ceremony. If you are 17 or 18, you will truly appreciate high drama and a good Passage party. You are in charge of this one. In your heart-mind, surround yourself with those in relationship who helped teach you about Women's Ways. Notice how your Mother let you go entirely or as much as she could. Observe this Passage ceremony as a lightning rod that will continue to inspire and ground you as you take off on your own.

You will remember the tutelage of new mentors as they appeared, and continue to appear.

What did you need from Mentors, Aunties and Grandmas before you left home? I can fill in the blanks on what I wish I had received, but what was true for you? Surround yourself with a ritual weekend or a week; invite, at least in your mind's eye, all the women who held you for these years of early development.

This time before the Sun sign changes is the perfect time to decorate your mask. If you agreed to meet with your Soul Sisters, oh my goodness, yes, do this together. Make your mask daring and beautiful to carry with you as you soar. All of your relationships, your young passions, your lessons, and your pain will be painted, feathered, glittered, and glued down to be symbolized in this mask. It becomes a most sacred object as this phase of your life ends in ritual.

Think high ritual. Shake your rattle. Once again, it's time to bid this stage of your life adieu. You have prepared, worked, even sweated to get your Soul-self ready to leave home. Invite one symbol for Death to pay you a good-time visit. Use the music of New Orleans to create an atmosphere for otherworldliness. You might even plan an overnight visit with your initiate Sisters and all of your Mentors if you want to. This time needs to be long enough to do a death lodge and make a clean delineation between the two halves of adolescence.

Sophia's mask, painted and feathered, daring and beautiful

You might ask, what is a death lodge? The persona of yourself at home, in your family space, surrounded by your parents' abundance and tens of thousands of memories will change forever. You will rewrap them and with your blessing allow them to fall back into the recesses of your body-mind.

Make a complete death ritual: As your pain is released, your action verb is transformation. All your confused emotions, even the high-lows and the low-highs, everything needs releasing except what belongs in your bundle. Invite intuition to come into this dance with creativity.

A death lodge could be easily created; maybe you all spread your sleeping bags out in wheel-spoke fashion, setting up drumming or music, then you climb into your bags for the duration. Your imagination needs no one's permission to create this for yourself, it's a ritual. Use what you have to create from the ground up, in ascending order. Be in the moment and try something new for the first time to weave a beautiful ceremony. If you want to trance dance, ask your initiates and wise-women to help create a space so you may all alter yourselves in safe ways. Perhaps you would use your mask and do a masked-trance-dance to an earthy drum beat. At the end of your frenzy get tucked inside your warm sleeping bag and cover your eyes. Go inside yourself and look back, look ahead. Please see how well this works, Soul Sisters. Remember this moment as powerful. Engage your own creative and intuitive powers. Make this ceremony one to remember and when it's over, it's over.

Women Who Run With the Wolves[15]

The psyches and souls of women also have their own cycles and seasons of doing and solitude, running and staying, being involved and being removed, questing and resting, creating and incubating, being of the world and returning to the soul-place.

-Clarissa Pinkola Estés

First Flight Threshold

LEAVING HOME

The last double dog dare explodes in your brain

You drive away, fly away teen!

Allow the magnificent universe to enter, taste everything

All at once, no barriers, no boundaries,

In free fall you're wise, wiser than your youth

At least until the daydream suggests otherwise.

Now you build your own nest, somehow feed yourself,

Seeking nourishment from unknowable places,

Dreaming slows you down but only a bit,

The hand of fate delivers Soul instructions.

Soul, your ever present, personal guide,

Rough-cut, you emerged at Birth to walk the Earth

For a lifetime of lessons, as a Soul-with-Purpose

If you listen, all of your gem facets will be polished.

You do your level best following, sweating, searching,

Not always out of control, quiet sometimes, listening

Wanting so much to just

Be you.

Please begin this section with a bit of solar plexus breath work, pumping your belly like an accordion as a way to enter deeply and honor your memories of all the days and seasons of the second half of your adolescence. Begin with eyes closed, candles lit, space set as you do. Maybe, hopefully, your ceremony to close out the first half of adolescence, fulfilled your need for party. Cross your First Flight threshold quietly when you feel ready. You are spreading your wings and falling off a cliff, waiting for the updrafts to catch you. Soar.

Remembering back to your life at the tender teen-ages of 17, 18, or 19, feel the natural combination of scared and competent. This is the weave of an independent spirit, now step away from home. Let go completely, you have a good plan laid out ahead. Stay with this young vision of yourself for as long as it takes to be her again.

Most women will have a persistent symbol or image of leaving home. My symbol was a Box Elder tree that I loved to climb. Many teen-age hours, I had escaped my big family to be alone up in her branches. I grew very teary when I said goodbye. I spent many days in that tree watching bugs, neighbors, and the sky. That Box Elder was my oldest and truest friend and I remember it leafed out the week I left home. I gave up a rooted friend who held my solitude when I climbed high into her branches for wheels to take me far away. In a single moment gripped by fate, I released one attachment for another. Because I was deeply wounded in early and middle adolescence, I graduated high school a year early and left home the day after graduation. I could not wait to leave. My Soul came knocking for me to cross the threshold, so I did.

Carefully consider how to review this long decade, 18 to 29. Your review will rise from this core of you, now well aged like a good wine. You may want to draw out a circular timeline that includes each season. What was your story from your late teens and early twenties? Would you like to understand that language of the Cosmos? Another approach to this mission may begin with biology, your adult brain matures around age 24. When that time arrived in your life, all cylinders inside your brain began firing together. You will find the late teens and early 20s differs considerably from the second half of the decade, the years 24 to 29. To look at 18 to 24 first, lay out all these years, 18-29 on a timeline, square or round, you choose. Maybe the date you left home is a personal anniversary. Once you do this the memories begin to flow.

Do you remember leaving home, being on your own, even moving in that direction? All those days make precious memories and will come back to you in waves if you stay quiet and openly ask memory to return. A gold mine of information about yourself is now buried in memories, how deep is it all buried? I like to go mining for the nuggets I consider golden, can you locate yours? No it's not all golden, but the shiny parts provide courage to help excavate the moldy, slimy parts. We all have both parts.

This review is meant to understand how the training and skills you gathered during this decade of your tender, early 20s has aligned with your Soul's purpose. Can you see how? Sit quietly with your actions, behaviors, thoughts, loves, scan your timeline and old photos; you will find clues to your deep inner core. Unless you were focused on these inner passions of your Soul, you were avoiding yourself. Can you remember your actions, your main decisions, and their reasons? Can you remember zoning out or numbing? There is little to focus on when you were not paying full attention, but search out times when you felt single-minded and in your power.

When you peer back into this part of your life, you will discover how your daring, adventurous self cared little for lengthy plans yet prepared you for everything that came after—your Adult and Elder arcs of life. Take special care to remember yourself, be tender and hold the facts without judgment. Write about how you spread your wings, how you opened to explore yourself and the world. Like everyone, you discovered a bit of humility through this first half of adolescence. There has been so much to learn. This was the time to experience mastery of one or two of your gifts. Write, write, the lessons come fast and furious during these years. I promise you will find nuggets of gold on this mining expedition.

As I guide you through this excavation, I want a candle nearby and your journal used well. Here come the thousand-thousand questions as I am compelled to ask. I do not know, so all I can do is ask. You are the one who knows everything about yourself. Hopefully reviewing will be revealing as well. Many Soul parts could have flown off during these ten or eleven long years. Look for those to return now.

When you moved beyond the confines of the nest and the confines of your nested mind, extraordinary things happened. Your mind turned into the cosmic receiver it actually was and felt ignited by your spirit guides, what happened? You are inside of First Flight, inside the bubble of your memories and thoughts, now.

For your writing pages: You may fanaticize or deal in stark reality, which do you choose? Was your first journey away from home a walk-about? No, hardly anyone on the planet does that anymore. Maybe you went on a round-the-world tour . . . what did you want so passionately when you spread your wings? Whatever you decided to do as your first independent action, did you choose well for yourself? Go into the quiet of your inner space and be with yourself at 18 and 19.

Keep asking: Who are you born to be? You might use your mask to reveal your needs to alter psychic tempo. Honor and remember how your glistening wings felt the first few times you used them. Did you do a dance between being and feeling like a young adult at one moment and not at all grown up in the next moment? Most women remember that dance, different days were different.

Stay as connected to Source, to the Divine Feminine as you are able. Strike up a conversation with the Womb of the Universe if you like; the only element of risk is openly sharing. Perhaps you dreaded that others would ridicule you; how did you protect your precious psychic experiences? Talking with your Mentor will keep you open to the sludge that needs to move out of your body. Did you talk with anyone about your life during these years?

Take an Eagle's view to consider this extraordinary decade from 18 to 29. These 4000 days as a young adult and still adolescent set the stage for your adult life. Peer into your memories. Your story is important and may take some time to recall and then re-story for the personal and private value that still resides there. Be as sweetly patient with yourself as you can be and consider how you walked along a developmental timeline. Did you truly get stuck in a few places? Be very tender if your find this to be true; once seen you may reveal patterns that need not be repeated. Your stories may feel confessional, exposing, and daringly revealing. Some stories may have taken a deep dive inside for long term hiding and pestering. Remain alert for any stickiness that may have led to arrested development.

My need to be loved and wanted, universal but hazardous, led me into a co-dependent relationship that taught many valuable, albeit painful lessons. I still rely on the skills that I polished during those first-marriage years. The pain landed me in the category of divorce, along with that baggage of shame. This is my Eagle's view.

After your adult brain finally matured at 24-25, did you embrace and align with your gifts? Did you dream sufficiently daring, sufficiently grand? Your Soul haunted you at impossible times if you tried to dodge your natural gifts. Look closely back on the impossible times, those times when the very breath and Soul of you may have closed around your possibilities like a knot around your life. Your Soul's calling may have disappeared completely. Was there some indecision when you found it harder and harder to say yes or no? Please add to your journal if you feel squishy or wiggly as your memories come alive. Do you remember your lessons? Did you repeat any?

You were born to grow and learn and produce good works. Your triune-self—body-mind-spirit with a triune brain, powerful beyond your imagination, layers together to reveal complexity—psychological and woundable. Sometimes it seems like everyone holds a clue but no one really feeds you. This reflection of your life is dreamy perhaps, even gossamer, then and now, only you can unlock your inner mystery. Finally out of school, you defined learning in ways that perfectly suited you. During this personal archeological dig, you may need strong intentions and fierce determination to continue. Always, your Soul led you through the rough spots. Even tough times were there for a reason. Your resilience grew stronger. Focus in on your gifts. Accompanying any rough spot, your most intense pain circles back to highlight growth and spotlight your gifts. I have come to think of pain as a community thing, I feel something of how others feel. This is like cosmic empathy. Besides, right next to your deepest wounds lies your greatest gifts.[6]

Did you find love to be irresistible and follow that thread for awhile? Maybe you entered college and followed a career path; did that lead to your spark? Perhaps you took that spark with you out of college and this review is a beautiful way to create a bonfire. We all fall for little children, perhaps that detour took you into parenting right out of the nest. No matter what this second half of adolescence did for you, you still have the spark, believe me, you do.

Pad the corners of your life with enough quiet to focus attention on your inner love. Follow your story through your timeline just as you have done from Birth. When you feel lost, remember you are resilient and a brilliant tracker of your inner self. Take time for a Moon ceremony to strengthen your resolve, smile, and launch on down the trail where the timeline thread leads. Because you are this many years old now, peering into the seasons ahead will be easier than all of the early stages. Now you know the signs and symbols of your Soul trying everything to get your attention. Even though you are chronologically closer to maturity, your trauma may or may not have been transformed. Now is the time. What happened to you during these years of your 20s? Only you can open this ritual to your Soul-self.

All of these questions are meant to prompt your pen: Write, write, write.

Maybe your journey connected dots between your relationships and teachers who came and went. Do you remember your next coach or mentor, and your next? How did you become teachable? As you connect with the teachings you gleaned through these unfolding years through your 20s, your bundle could overflow. Remember those tiny treasures, the gifts you have already placed into your sacred bundle. How do your earlier discoveries feed into your seasonal discoveries of this decade? Do you want to bow to or honor your helpers in a ritual or writing?

Alchemy works the interior space of the psyche, which lies between the inner relationship of your ego personality and the core of yourself, your Soul. Pay attention to this. Hold the realization that something inside shimmers. You're a woman, like all women, you have many facets. Put your focus again on your Soul-self. Pause. Who was this beautiful young woman and how did she find her way? How did she identify the path that belonged to her alone? Finally, this is alchemy, how does all that growth and transformation of your former selves affect who you are today?

Perhaps this great search yields depth and purpose in clear and crisp terms. As your mind tunes into your Soul's intuition and your body's receptivity, you will begin to feel the Cosmos too. Sometimes I feel the Cosmos in my intuition, like a download, other times a shiver travels up my spine. Still other times, the Cosmos delivers goose-bumps to verify someone's truth. Yes you are, we all are, made of stardust and so is your elusive Soul. This finer attunement is what we all want, we want to be on purpose, we long to align with what we are uniquely designed to do.

I call this transformative force that belongs to everyone, Source connection. This eternal part lives through you as Soul and deserves your focus now. You might find this a useful meditation while you review your last days of adolescence: "As above, so below, like the outside, so the inside." The thread of your Soul leads to your Cosmic Consciousness. Soul is the essence of this recovery. Doing ritual, staying close to the quiet will bring harmony to this new weave of all your ages and stages. Experiences begin as energy, but store away as nano-neurons of memory. Somewhere, perhaps locked inside of your many transformations, your memory thread leads straight from then to now, to who you are exactly, before your 30th birthday.

There are many parts of you; every archetype you rediscover makes you more whole. All these parts really want your cerebrum to recognize the gifts that remain locked up in your Soul. An area of growth worth exploring is your personal and accumulated archetypes. Do you know your archetypes? These are patterns that repeat as your natural, many faceted self. These patterns can be fascinating ways to view yourself. I have found teachings on archetypes in Clarissa Pinkola Estes' vast storytelling library on SoundsTrue.com,[15] in Carolyn Myss' *Sacred Contracts*,[16] and a grand little book by Jean Shinoda Bolen, *Goddesses in Older Women: Archetypes in Women over Fifty*.[17] To examine your archetypal patterns, turn your heart to that moment when you climbed a tree and looked down on your life or when you left home. Look for the hand of fate, that which turned you or kept you on your path. To search out these patterns, follow your timeline.

On Halloween, were you a gangster or a goof? You might have been a goth, a hippie, a witch, or a priest. Most of us tried out the prostitute, the rebel, and the victim archetypes. Some of these images will spark others. Somewhere within this decade, your archetypes settled into particular Soul shapes. Which ones have been revealed as your very own? Where did your passions catch fire? How did you respond to fiery passions? When you find these patterns, they will help introduce your Passage to Adulthood.

Adulthood arrives with the end of the second half of adolescence, after age 29 and close enough to 30 to call that your threshold. Something happened: What was your catalyst for change?

I recently heard someone say, Saturn with all his rings, slowly floats through the Cosmos. Just after your 29th birthday, Saturn realigns to its place at the time of your Birth. Decked out with sticky notes on the rings, Saturn comes around to remind you what you were born to do and who you were born to be. Saturn's operating manual comes at the end of your adolescence to set your adult self on a clear and unhindered path. Often responsibilities come into stark focus. Can you visualize those sticky notes, turning in the Cosmos? Saturn is an energy gently reminding you that your Soul came with a mission on the day you were born. Did a strong message come through here for you at this time, age 29 or 29.5? Who were you born to be? What was the big event before Saturn returned in your birth chart? I hope the worldly experience of your Saturn return, just before you turned 30, offered notable and memorable drama.

Locked inside of two archetypes, the prostitute—literally giving myself and my Soul away to corporate slavery and serial boyfriends—and adventurer, I found myself looking up at Saturn's rings and the breathtaking skyscrapers of New York City. With my personae intact, the Idaho tomboy and the daring adolescent, I welcomed my Womanhood Bloom as a total stranger in a strange land. Saturn came around precisely on time, like another hand of fate in my life. The return of Saturn rocked me and my world to its core.

I agree with those who claim the arrival of adulthood is marked by this Saturn return. After those 29.5 years of wanting and searching for the threshold of Womanhood Bloom, the energy of this time is unmistakable. Yes, it's also true that Saturn returns again before you turn 60 to remind you again, although your Soul message may be different for your Elder years than for your adult years. It is also true that the arc ahead, the adult years, will last 29 or 30 years.

Contrarians object to this view until they pass the adulthood threshold by a year or so. After age 30 or 32, nearly unanimous agreements are made about this threshold for womanhood and manhood. For most of us in the Western world psyche, adulthood spreads over us when we turn 30 and demands our whole attention.

Since you have renewed your relationship with the Child and the Youth parts of yourself, you could possibly speak or write your Soul's mission. Of your personal operating manual held by Saturn, what do you affirm? By the time you arrive at this place on your timeline, can you describe your operating manual?

Isn't it fun to think about? How much has this reflection helped in your review of your life's path? I have been through tough knotholes myself. If this has not been entertaining or you do feel stuck, please seek a local healer who can help you unstick. If you feel in any way incomplete, go find a new teacher; someone may be holding the other end of your string.

Observation of this time of your life was as worthy then as now. You may wish to pause to do a vision quest, to take an adventure of a lifetime, a walk-about, or a long trek. Maturity is not a given, everyone's journey is unique, but pausing to attend to and remember your Soul's calling will better prepare you for the great arc of adulthood ahead.

Because you began at the very beginning to step yourself down memory lane and because you have now honored all the past events without judgment, something else happened. You found love for your little self, for your scared self, for your daring self, and for your shame. Along this spirit trail, you have learned humility, wonderment, deep forgiveness, and peace in the process.

This pilgrimage back through your days certainly helps open you and causes Wow[18] to be an operative prayer: You did all that and survived, you walked and talked through the trauma and the joy. As Dr. Clarissa Pinkola Estés says in her Prayer for Traveling the Mother Road, "Thank you Madre Grande. Aymen. Aymen. Aymen. (and a little woman.)"[19]

Honor your memory with art. Have you sparked a Soul errand? Stick to that spark, write it, color it, dream it. That was you remembering something you came here to give, to do, to be. Since you are here, dancing yourself at 29 or 30 around to your present self and your present age, begin to tend that spark if it is the true fire of you, the piece you came to retrieve. Place that spark in a bed of soft down from a cattail and feed little chips of wood until it flames. Rather than allow the spark to rest, take yourself to movement, to dance, to modern jazz. Blow life into it!

Before maturity, adolescents take risks that no adult would consider taking yet the rewards come through the experience. Sift through all the layers. Take time to heal what you find that still hurts. Search out disappointments in cast-off gifts. Your gifts, formerly cast off, need to be clasped to your breasts. Breathe in those found gifts. Reclaim the pieces of your Soul you carved away while you were seeking approval or love.

Death Rattle. This ritual belongs to you and can take any form. Bringing gifts for the end of your adolescence, welcome Saturn and Raven. Invite them in. Laughing, Raven comes round like Saturn turns, but offers different rules. Raven asks you to drink caffeine, lay down, roll yourself up in a blanket or shroud and rest into a death lodge to release this time of your life. The Sun sign is about to change, your review of joy and pain for your adolescent self comes to its natural end. You need to simply let your adolescent self float down the river of life into the sea. Rest. Release. Take all the time you need. If different than Raven, invite your symbol for Death to pay you a good time visit. Plan an overnight visit with your initiates and all of your mentors if you are able to. This time needs to be long enough to do a death lodge and make a clean delineation between the end of this second half of adolescence and the beginning of adulthood. Make a complete death ritual so all of your pain is released, your action verb is transformation. Allow your confused emotions, as before the highs and the lows, to burn through the metamorphosis of transformation, alchemically revealing what belongs in your bundle.

Bundle Gathering. Have you gathered clues to place in your bundle? Have you spent your time well during this part of your pilgrimage? It feels good to be complete with all of your adolescence. Applaud your good work, show off your updated art portfolio. You might consider starting a new journal. The whole southern half of the Life Spiral ends in this death lodge. You might want to place that old journal in your sacred bundle and begin a brand new one for Adulthood.

Shake your rattle, once again, it's time to bid this stage of your life adieu. You are ready to embrace the power of Womanhood. This work is bringing you to an entirely new consciousness about your life. You now see the first 30 years through a developmental lens. You have worked through my Coyote questions and taken great notes for your autobiography. Plan to take time for this later, the stories of your life are important to all who love you. Storytelling is rising in the culture as the new folk psychology, perhaps you find the thread back to your Ancestors' fire circle. Telling your stories provides stellar opportunities to heal; we will see much more of this in the future.

This pause is for you to give birth to an inner shaman; you need time to coalesce everything you have discovered. Yes, you are on your way to becoming an initiated Elder, one of the rarest of the rare in our culture. My women friends have helped me become a careful culture watcher. We have talked for decades about cultural repair, malaise, and transformations. Everyone who ever looked outside still benefits from looking inside where we commune with our Soul. Within your Soul is God, the Genius of the Universe, all that you ever needed is there. I want you to look inside for your wholeness. When you were born you came in whole. In this place where you stand, your Womanhood threshold, you have recovered parts and gifts that will return you to wholeness.

In the past months, you have marched to a drum beat we created together. How does your drum beat, now, just for you? Change anything you wish. Over this threshold, my process continues with questions for your writing pages and reminders to watch the Moon and the Sun to remake your world round. By elongating this process giving you space, inviting you to experience freedom, I hope you recognize your inner shaman's need to be, to instigate, and to find spaciousness in your life.

Your ceremonies need to be intentional and celebratory. What is life if not a celebration, and out of the box at that? Be ingenious, be your own Genius. Begin to live your unbelievable life as you own the rituals and the good directions that brought you this far. Begin now to declare your own design.

A good time to rest. No matter where you live in Spiral chronology, I invite you to take a long rest. I recommend a spa break here to breathe, to play really hard, to do art, to allow some of your discoveries to settle into your triune-self, and to formalize what you believe. Perhaps you define a rest as a weekend or a month, you are the weaver.

"Each Birth story includes hints of an inner myth trying to enter the world through us. We are mythic by Nature, each carrying the thread of a unique plotline that seeks to unfold throughout the course of life. At critical junctures, be it a great challenge, a devastating loss or radical change in life, the story of the Soul tries to break through and become more conscious. For, the human Soul needs an outer drama in order to reveal its inner myth."

-Michael Meade from mosaicvoices.org[6]

Praying for your womanhood

Womanhood Bloom Threshold

I say welcome to your Adult Threshold. Congratulations! Chronologically, you have arrived at the threshold of Womanhood. You have moved through Birth to Middle Child to First Blood and First Flight, zero to thirty. Steeped in ceremony I invite you to breathe in the pregnant future of your life, right here.

Of course at this juncture, your biological development ceases because all of your systems have fully matured. Beliefs created by you serve only you. In your belief system do you find space for fate and destiny? Can you believe in your Soul's guidance? Can you feel the imprint of the Great Mystery on your life? In the midst of tragedy and even terror, can you find room for "there are no accidents" and "you chose this path before you were born?" I admit this takes us out of our box of smallness and launches us into the Cosmos. At 60 or 70 some part of you knows these answers. Did you know when you turned 30?

If you are 30-something, slow way down for a few moments. *Soul Stories* was designed by 3Beauties, each 35. When this Womanhood Bloom threshhold was reached, they rested, quiet and in awe of this process.

If you are 30-something, I wrap my Elder arms around you with this suggestion: Stop here. Read the 3Beauties story in Part III. Allow this remembering time to be your ordeal, the next trip the Earth makes around the Sun: This next year is your initiation. Enjoy being one of the few. Think about who you know that needs to take this pilgrimage. Share.

Woman, you have traveled a very long way through your story line to be in this moment! May we breathe together before we plunge back in? Let's welcome all the women who have taken time to birth babies, anywhere along their timeline. You Mothers have had your own initiation, set apart from your developed life as you grew bulbous, and then as you coddled your newborn. As you looked down into your babe's eyes, thoughts swirled. Please take time to be with that threshold, whenever it was, however it was for you. For the generations who follow us on this pilgrimage, you will ensure they have something more in their lives.

Still, as rare as a bird in a winter storm, a woman's ceremony is something to respect, to hold in awe and in wonderment. I have helped quite a few women celebrate this Threshold of Womanhood. I want a thousand-million women to have initiation ceremonies, but I settle for the seeds we can plant together.

Crossing into 30 feels remarkably profound; its impact on the decade that follows is equally profound. Here is where your woman-power begins to build, your inner knowledge, your way of dreaming your life and your family's life, connections moor you to life. Each year builds on the one before, every season builds these early years. These next two decades lay out for your review but seem to stretch farther than your mind can fathom. Notice this stage where you literally stand on your Womanhood Threshold looking backward with an exhale and forward with an inhale. You are a flower, inner and outer, and you have a bloom.

Please begin slowly with a candle and quiet. Notice the lightness you feel from your death lodge ceremony. You released every growing up pain, so I feel you have arrived. Do you agree? You have a blank journal or at least a blank page to begin. Since we are remembering, I will join in. With my palms pressed together, I acknowledge a thousand-thousand teachers who have influenced my journey. They are teachers without hooks. Most of them flowed into me from a book or an audio, or peeked out of a sister's story. "When the student is ready, the teacher will appear." This saying has kept me primed for the very next one who showed up. I feel gratitude for the whole landslide of teachers and regret that I didn't go deep with every single one.

Who were your teachers? Who broadened your horizon? Perhaps you are still holding a curiosity that a teacher may fulfill. Do you recall the magnetism you felt that drew a teacher to you? Was it intention, desire, a prayer, or an accident?

Writing pages. Here come your questions for this first half

be these years to yourself chrono- akes order out of your thousand te a bubble map to visually assist u choose for yourself? What were his story of what you did and what ionships help define you? How do oday? What were your woundings? the answers, perhaps. Take your

for these ages, 30 to early 50s, I se I have set you free and you are ow, you will decide when to cross get, the more our differences shine en remotely alike. The Diné wom- he maturity of womanhood comes knowing. Holding this for myself, ace of years that was an awakening, ma. By age 52, I felt every bit the rue Elder self. At 52, I even trav- eled across the Three Mesas of Hopi land and to Navajo land to sit beside old women. In your reflection, you will see for yourself how poignant and profound moments marked your life.

Did your values shift as you found your footing as an adult with responsibilities that fit your stage of development? What were your special coping mechanisms? In every year there are highs and lows, can you chronicle the seasons for yourself in terms of thrills and disappointments?

For this pilgrimage of remembering, can you take over for this mad-coyote-woman and wonder about how your timeline unfolded? What led to what? Lay out your timeline and tell your story well during this next month. Do you want to plan a day to gather with your initiate Sisters and your Mentor to share this early Womanhood story? Does any part of it penetrate into your life today? Focus on how.

Beliefs. You are grown now, so it's time to be gentle and walk yourself through the core issue of beliefs beyond life and death. I saved beliefs about everything for adulthood, so this is me, being on purpose. By now, your opinions have been shaped by wind and water forces—yours and others. Please be tender with yourself, or be fierce with yourself, for inner peace your beliefs need resolution. Walking and writing, these tools belong to this moment, right now.

If you have grandchildren this challenge may be interesting, frustrating, or too much like school. Write at length about what you believe and how "involved" actively or psychically you feel about the state of the world: climate change, mass extinction, philosophy and religion, politics. You need to know what you think to engage your teenage grandchildren. This conversation with yourself is your gift to them.

You have already started. Check and see if you are clear: What do you believe about life and death? What do you believe about the Divine, the Source, the Creator or Great Mystery? Is God your name for this entity? What do you believe about your aspects, are you really body and Soul? Have you ever experienced out-of-body time and space? Have you lived past lives? Why did you choose your parents? Do you create your own reality? If so, how? What role does the hand of fate play? Did you come to Earth with a destiny? Please find your inner clarity for these terms: Soul, psyche, Ancestors, guides, consciousness, fate, and destiny.

There are thousands of possible combinations to these questions, but you have come bravely through the last six months and I ask you to up your courage now. Allow your Soul-self to catch up to your left brain reasoning and your right brain creativity. What you believe is totally up to you. No one needs to be pleased by you following something that is not true in your core. You deserve to find the truth in knowing what you know and feeling the confidence of your whole being click-in with affirmation and recognition.

Meditate. Do ritual for no reason. Read through your notes. Do a thorough task of examining your long search for gifts and Soul pieces. Please add to my list of questions. You might sit quietly and make a sacred bundle that will contain the recovered bits of you found along this spirit trail. How do you put yourself back together now? Do you need your initiation sisters, or one other to perform a shamanic ritual, to feel whole? Is it possible you have not stopped yet with the slicing off Soul parts?

I know that my fragmentation did not stop until I was 44. Perhaps you begin to see why gathering this is so important. Life stunts us when we are not looking. My maturity stopped along the timeline even though time continued. Before I knew this for certain, I was so far beyond this Womanhood threshold I was almost standing on a different threshold. Perhaps you also awakened later in life. I was 46 when I invited a shamanic ritual to put me all together. Soul sometimes needs extra drama. When I shattered my body at age 49, I needed a soul retrieval ritual to feel whole again. Throughout this decade of change my Soul really wanted me to awaken.

You are familiar now with how certain rituals draw out your memories, especially the deeply immersed timed writings. I hope you have enjoyed this rhythm and found it workable in your life. Continue on as you have, morning or evening pages, Moon rituals, Nature walks, moving through all the memories of being an adult woman. You have crossed five thresholds and spent quality time in the space between them. Once again you find yourself in betwixt and between time, the broad expanse of shimmering space between thresholds. For only one month, unless you choose more, this liminal space will reveal its transformative essence because you hold your memories lightly and fondly. Have you discovered that each season holds a different flavor, a different energy for you?

How shall we work with these metaphors, the spring time and summer time of life, your child and youthful selves? They have alchemically melted into your being at this spiral place which makes adulthood so very strong and mysteriously deep with your stories. Do you observe Medicine Wheel teachings in your belief system? Enveloping the span and all your stories from these two full stages of development now gives you a feel for the speed of the Earth turning around the Sun. The Earth is moving at unbelievable speeds, over 67,000 miles per hour around our day star the Sun. We begin to understand why it feels that life moves so fast. Our living planet and her different energies around the solar year offer such different flavors for your meditation.

I ask you to remember **6000** days of living in a single month because we have a destination, you and I. Re-enact, honor and remember the years that moved you from thirty to the place you know as the middle when something else appeared. In that middle, the threshold ahead, your middle adult phase called forth her own essence. Spend time with each of your birthdays from now to this next edge. There are highlights embedded in all of these years between thresholds. Those highlights are rich and worthy of your blessed memories. I invite you to remember! Write! Walk! Repeat!

You received blessings from each of these years allowing you to learn what? Do what? Experience what? Stay in your beginner's mind to be able to repeat these questions for each full turn of the Earth around the Sun. Your Soul held your attention and fate guided you through all of these teachings. Remember what it felt like to be you. I hope renewed gusto awakens you every day and you catch a dream that brings you a message. The more attention you pay to your dreams the more active your dream life will become. Allow the memories stirred by this gusto to flow into your journal.

By now, you feel the rhythm of the Moon as your own. As before, watch how the phases of the Moon invite you out for your Medicine Walks. New-Half-Full-Half. This is an invitation, because you tuned in, you feel her energy now. She pulls on your water. When you feel this energy, ask if there are Soul messages waiting for you. Use your own practice and sing songs that you loved from this time. What was hot? Improve on my version of ritual to review this super-charged adult time of your life.

Create an unforgettable event with your initiate sisters, maybe a sleep-over where you talk all night long. You can search out your Soul parts together and the wounds needing attention. Maybe you will locate the memories that attach to your inner gifts. The exploration of this entire early adult phase seems to blow your mind. Notice everything about your daydreams, this and that happened, did you intend, dream, imagine, or bet on any of it happening like it did? Oh my, do you have journals to review? I double-dog dare you to spend an afternoon as a treat to your Soul-self. What will you do, just for your Soul?

I believe we live mythological lives with too little awareness. At every age your Soul-self delivers outrageous challenges: What was the challenge you accepted at this time of your life? A major component of Rites of Passage in mythology, in history, and in practice is an ordeal. In your story, your ordeal may only need to be reframed to recognize its true nature. Even without a way to celebrate your growth, did you live through a personal heroine's story? What did you accomplish that shines in neon behind your eyelids?

Just when you were relaxing in cruise-control, your guides and your Soul quite naturally led you into restlessness, a twist of fate that seems invisible until you discover yourself seeking more of something. Do you remember moments of longing? Did your life need clarity or a different pace? What were you thirsty for when the word change entered your vocabulary again? Shake your rattle dear little Soul-self, another threshold looms. This one ahead is the training ground of all training grounds.

Have you mined the riches from this time of your Woman-hood Bloom? Have you gathered your gifts and your Soul parts back to your heart-mind? Through deep reflection on my persistent questions, you have become the storyteller of your life. Your Soul Story continues until you feel joyfully ready to share from your deep well of discovery.

If you feel complete with this stage and ready to release, ready to accept the transformation that is yours, lie down with your Soul Sisters for a ritual to close out this first half of your adult time—so long, so rich, and so deep. Gather your ritual elements, gather your relations, gather your reclaimed Soul parts. Close this door so you may welcome the next door opening. Shake that death rattle as you bid your thirties farewell along with some part or all of your forties.

You've written memories for your Bloom and you've established a strong, personal belief system that feels comfortable. Successes and failures brought lessons for your inner judge. You've brought your ordeal into the light to see it for what it was. All this gives you a couple of insightful companions for the next stages of life—at eighteen competence travelled with you, now you have added confidence and woman-power. You know what you know and nothing can take that from you.

Every stage has challenges, bring them on! You can say that now and mean it. Consider what you have completed before you open yourself to review the next stage of your life. Pause. Reflect. Aren't you a Phenomenal Woman? Oh God, thank you for Maya Angelou!

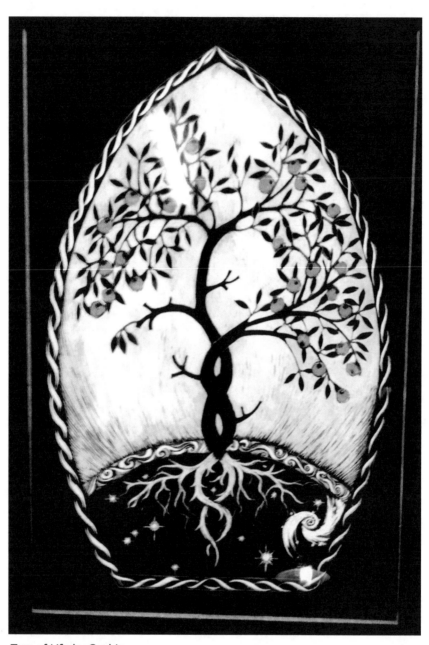

Tree of Life by Sophia

Deepening Womanhood Threshold

Deepening Womanhood, this very Middle-of-your-Life, flows naturally from and beyond your Womanhood threshold. Clasp your sacred bundle of Soul parts, your healed wounds, to your breast and step across the threshold.

Remember back to that moment that lasted only a flash because Saturn returned at 29.5 and moved along by 30; look at the incredible expanse of experience and knowledge that has come into you since then. Saturn will return again later in this stage of your life to ask—what did you come to do? Always and gently, Saturn keeps you in this question. The second Saturn return is what solidified my Elder years. Remember, Saturn comes around to remind you of the question at 59, but your Soul holds the answers, now, now!

You will see and feel that this mid-life threshold for Deepening was marked with a profound longing. Lean into that longing to find your answers: Your Deepening threshold indicates the embrace of your life, a thirst for something extraordinary. This longing is Soul knocking, asking, what more do you want from life? I hope you know exactly what I refer to when, in your silence, you hear the knocking, an urgency to fulfill your dreams. How do you respond to this deep longing?

I wish to elevate your experiences at this time of your life. Claim the birth of your wisdom-self right now. This quality has been building since childhood. When you peer into the collection of days and thresholds in your rear view mirror, you are a mighty wise woman. You will be rewarded, maybe even surprised how you laid the foundation for wisdom for all the years ahead.

"You are valuable and so is the wisdom you hold." Several times my women friends said those words to me, when I turned 50 and again as I turned 60. Nothing else mattered because their beautiful words rang through my dreams. May I turn those words to you now, "You are valuable and so is the wisdom you hold."

I would like to hold your heart in my hands for just a moment. This is the time when your parents will begin to let go of the things they love. Most of all, they love you and your children. You are the last thing your parents will let go of and vice-versa. May we all find good ways to let go. Perhaps one more eulogy—finding the source for your parents as superheroes—could be considered before you take another step into this Deepening.

Relationships play a part in each woman's development. Your parents brought their gifts and gave them wholeheartedly. Who are we to judge how the gifts were delivered? Most of that is history and can be processed if you need more time. Look for the hooks in your parental relationships. If you need professional attention, more than your Mentor can offer, ask an energy worker or a therapist for help.

Remember, be gentle with yourself! Look at the conditions you were born into. Those conditions set you off on this quest. You have the power to reinterpret past experiences through a new perspective—to gain a better understanding of what is guiding you forward. What impulse makes you passionate? How do you summarize your mid-life turn? Who was there with you?

I found it necessary to reinvent myself at this threshold and I was thrilled that my reflection back into these years now far behind me, provided motivation for the years ahead of me. What I held fast to was the belief that every cell would renew and I would claim an all new identity. I was finished with my life as a corporate cog. I had not yet settled into my comfortable belief system about life and death, but I was clear life held out mystery and mastery for me to claim. Being who I am, heart and Soul, I knew that meant 10,000 hours of studying and then 10,000 more hours of solidifying. Such sacred intentions are incredibly powerful; it wasn't long, maybe 5 years into the project and I felt so wholly new I was a completely different woman.

Your ritual now emerges from a practiced groove. Create time to review these years, maybe 45 to 60, maybe 50 to 65. You know. With our elongating lifespans, 52 seems an odd threshold for some, especially those who plan to live long into their 90s and 100s. Women's extreme individuation means none of these later thresholds come at a set time. But they can be felt, which is why I say, you know. All the next thresholds come on your time rather than the number of your solar returns. You will know, I promise.

Relocate your celebratory quiet. Alter your mood by inviting a high-holy space. Create a time warp for deep listening. Your spiritual inclination may invite renewed curiosity to explore this time. I hope you have fallen in love with the surprises that have arrived by unlocking Spirit's mystery. Remember, oh please remember the moments when your inner power stepped you into the light so magnificent you moved forward. Consider how this happened for you during mid-life, a sacred time of life filled with wisdom and energy.

With an edginess of change and a longing to embrace transformation, life asks you for a recommitment. Your wise-woman inside traversed the past decades in the trenches—often soaring, often sweating. By grace and grit, you have learned so much. I feel grateful you have come this far reviewing your life's Soul Story. I place a spotlight here for your mid-life change, because my own seemed so dramatic.

Whenever I do reflect on everything that happened to me in these years, I feel struck with awe. Twists of fate pointed me toward my destiny—everything caused my focus to turn inward. Because I was seeking, the Universe cooperated with my Soul. Twenty years later, reading *Fate and Destiny* by Michael Meade,[6] I found myself re-reviewing my own time of Deepening because he described so well my twists of fate; my Soul was alert and participating. When I read his book, I chuckled in amazement.

My way is to throw questions at you. For this review I will offer questions as before, believing those may be helpful. First, I want to emphasize the glory in the personal drama of your life. As you turn your attention to this review, take or leave my guidance, but draw out every one of your pearls of wisdom. Those pearls belong to you! Those precious pearls surround your essence which coalesce to make you wise!

The frontiers of retirement, grandparenting and coping with an aging body, all these headlines lie ahead. Think in terms of personal, fulfilling, and preparatory. You could unpack those three adjectives like writing challenges: What did you find personal, what was fulfilling, and what happened to prepare you for the time ahead?

Midway through this very adult expression of you, notice all of your restless stirrings. Some event may have triggered something still unfulfilled from your Soul. Enter into the stillness inside to find the courage to dive into your memories. Give yourself time to be artful with your timeline of events. This may be the age and stage Clarissa Pinkola Estés was speaking of when she recorded *The Late Bloomer*.[15] She is talking if you will listen.

As the age begins to show through our laugh lines, sisterhood grows in importance, blood sisters and sisters in spirit. For this month-long review of your recent history, you may need extra time with your initiate sisters. Look forward to some outrageous laughter as you share reviews. Life is always offering more and each phase of life is a preparation for the next.

Just like all the others, this time of your life was filled with lessons. Here comes the litany of questions for your journal. I hope to stir fabulous autobiographical pages and help you reassemble your Soul parts.

What was your unfinished business that poured over from the first half of your adult experience? What stopped you from reaching for that star, the one holding your great aspirations, your biggest dreams? What are your most cherished memories along this timeline? Where did sorrow and suffering take you? How did you emerge from prideful or shameful moments?

Does it help to remember the seasons within your years? Are the answers to your burning questions locked inside old journals, perhaps? In review, after you received the wake-up call for this new stage in life, what did you do? Your identity battle was completely over. Maybe, like me, you just wanted a new one. If you felt ready to experience wholeness, did the next teacher suddenly appear or did you embark on a search? Who has been your most enduring teacher? Did you recommit to your business? Did you change careers or continue on for your 30 year investment? Did future retirement or a new adventure show up as more important?

The cosmic knock to alert another level of consciousness may have been a startling wakeup or a subtle nag. No doubt, some drama stirred your mid-life marker. Searching to meet up with your Soul, you certainly have no time to be bored. Something stirs again and again. What stirred you awake to your life as you approach your seventh decade? What sustaining energy will push you across your Elder threshold? Are you willing or not? As always the oracles, Astrology, Tarot, I-Ching may be consulted to take your current observations to a new level of awareness. Do you align most days with your purpose or do you still need to lay your claim?

Does your spiritual practice need a tune-up? What caused you to slowly uncoil the kundalini energy? Was it an empty nest plus or minus a couple of years? Did you start something your Soul would not allow you to put off any longer?

We women especially, but men also, have great needs to feel comfortable, important, and loved. How did you sustain your need to feel loved? Do you walk differently because of an awakening? How can you honor your life lessons? Now is the time. Have you realized how much you are a Soul-guided body?

When you spend time reviewing your lessons of these years, do you see that you have long been headed for your Elder years, is this destiny or has denial been playing with you? How did you deepen the bloom of your Womanhood?

It may be good to spend this Sun sign in the luxury of re-membering how you laid a foundation for growing gracefully into the aging process. Light your candles, mark your calendar, honor the last drops of your Blood. Whether your Moontimes came regularly or not matters little as you review this time. I invite you to recreate a sacred energy to envelop your bleeding times; summon good, deep Moon meditations. Watch how Grandmother Moon moves through every day of this Sun sign. Her drum beat, Full-Half-New-Half happens with blessed regularity. With only intuition to guide you, you might create a Moon-altar for your pause time. Bring to your mind the gratitude that opened in you when your hot flashes ended. Grandmother Moon now only regulates your water retention and release. She is always there for you.

I invite you to story your experience, now, First Blood to Last Blood. Do this for your granddaughters. They want and need to hear your way of treating Blood as sacred.

This mid-point in your adulthood is the most important space between the two thresholds, the previous crossing into adulthood and the future one, embracing Elderhood. Your time, here and now, in the middle begs for a celebratory review. Your life may be half over, but it's your life to celebrate. Passages are tied to Soul rather than chronology. Obviously, once you reached 30 you were ready for adulthood, but often elderhood doesn't even arrive at 60, because women are heart-full, young and vigorous. Also women take denial as far as they can go with it. Elder is a concept that badly needs an image makeover. Many will simply wave as Saturn comes back around, please heed the question, who were you born to be? Only cross your Elder Threshold on your own timeline. This is the highest honor of your life and one of modeling for every woman younger than you. Be authentic to your Soul.

Angeles Arrien, one of our culture's most beloved Elders, wrote *The Second Half of Life: Opening the Eight Gates of Wisdom*.[4] As either a book or a soulful recording, this is a treasure worth exploring from SoundsTrue.com. In it she offers how this Passage, Deepening Womanhood, invites you to explore how you might use creativity to leave a lasting legacy for you community. In this Passage, you understand how all of your previous roles prepare you for the Elder role ahead. Rising like cream, your authenticity meets your courage. Nature gives you deep solace and provides incentive to care for your body. I personally think the invitation into new experiences feels like the intersection of thirty and sixty. I recommend Angie to you and your journey; she is a lasting source of inspiration in my life.

Since this is a review of recent history, all the seasons want to be coaxed into stark appraisal. Let's adopt Byron Katie's phrase, *Loving What Is*,[21] her book title holds the essence of this liminal time. As she advises, let's tell the truth. Stay with the writing pages as if your life will be revealed. It has been, truly all those pages have been filled with your very life. This is the transformative key, the truthful story of your Soul, your Soul Story. Watch this transformation in action, your mind begins to operate with more kindness, more love. You are getting closer to your wholeness with every passing day. Are you beginning to see the wholeness in the pattern of your character? Often one must pass midlife to see the character that has been building from Birth.

A FINE LITTLE PRACTICE OF HONORING

Michael Margolis's Superhero Exercise, to make each one of us better storytellers:[20]

Get a blank piece of paper (landscape): draw a line down the middle

On the top left side of the piece of paper write MOTHER

On the top right side of the piece of paper write FATHER

Answer these three questions:

If you had to describe these personalities, what would be the snapshot picture of how they are in the world?

What were the gifts that your mother / father figure gave you?

What were the things that they didn't teach that you wish they had, that you hoped they would have provided to you, that you had to figure out yourself/find somewhere else?

Be with your emotions. Are you holding onto regrets or sorrows? Search out their truth. Does it help to re-read Sue Monk Kidd's quote or the positive recognition and gratitude offered by Angeles Arrien? Whenever something has come to my attention that needs to be released, I discover a weight attached that has stopped my forward movement, I can barely slog through the heavy energy. When I slow down to attend and dissolve some piece of shame or regret, my world brightens considerably. Is this true for you?

Teachers are abundant. In Byron Katie's book, *The Work*[21] is well detailed with methods to come clean and love your truth. That was a tall order for me because I did indeed have some work to do. After doing my own process mixed with hers and talking in circle, I feel spacious and free of hooks and barbs that had haunted me for years. Some hooks had a Soul piece attached. Reclaiming my truth provided freedom from what held me back as my Soul revealed yet another twist of fate. This is your life, it can be loved and only made better by exploring and reclaiming your authentic self. It is possible to relax into gratitude for simply being on the receiving end of all those lessons.

As you grow closer to Now, you begin to see your Divine wholeness at the end of this pilgrimage. Your Moon walks may take on a new quality. You may discover such a true spiritual connection with Nature that you feel drawn outside no matter what the weather because you must breathe the gift from the trees. I invite you to notice how ritual breathes you as you breathe the trees. You will begin to coalesce.

I like this word, coalesce, because of its sensate meaning: To become one in growth. It derives directly from its Latin version, coalescere, from the 1540s "to unite, grow together." When your body feels the need to be with Nature then you have grown much closer to your true self; you discover the peace you have searched for all your life. Nature is inviting, even in a storm. Her invitation directs you to feel united with yourself. In Nature you are able to practice what you believe without defense, without discussion. What you believe is between you and God and the Divine you discover inside yourself especially when you are outside. You are beginning to coalesce with the Earth, our Great Mother, and with all that is.

While it's true that this Deepening time of your adult life was long and worthy of a thorough review, it comes to a natural end as did all the other turns around the Life Spiral. The next threshold approaches. Only one thing will coax this beautiful time to end and that is another beautiful time. Ahead is your Elder Encore. Actually three thresholds lie ahead. There you will discover an ease in gathering wisdom from all of your years and turns through the seasons.

Observe the energy of Saturn's return for the second time. Ask someone with deep experience in Astrology to explain your own Saturn return to you. We surround ourselves with the smartest women we know. At your Elder threshold an entire arc of life awaits as do great adventures. My assignment to gather enough experience to be an authority has caused me to lead many initiations over the past two decades. I ask you to see my hands clapping because you have gathered enough experience to be an authority in many ways by living through your age of complexity, this Deepening Womanhood. Be sure you find time to mine your deep experiences and time to bundle the Soul slices recovered and the gifts discovered: Lay out all your findings in art and memories.

As the neuro-pathways have laid a practiced groove, you live ritual now. There will always be moments when your inner power steps you into the light to reveal your magnificence to all your relations. Consider how this happened for you at this mid-life arc. Truly this time of your life is so sacred and filled with wisdom and energy.

May I say to you with my whole heart, the most important time of your life lies ahead. The most of every category lies ahead. Perhaps, like me, you are not quite sure where your bounce went, but that is the only thing I miss from all the days of my life before 60. Many of my friends still have their bounce, although their boundless bounce causes me to scratch my head in wonder. Gravity affects all of us in unique ways.

The times we live, in this 21st Century, are challenging and each one of us has our personal list of crises that need immediate attention. Elder becoming, the demands on your wisdom to solve these challenges has never been greater. Be in your most reverent and graceful posture to celebrate this threshold ahead. Give adulthood a nod to come along, truly there are tendrils of your whole life that follow you into your wisdom years. Your library is inside of you, your photo albums are in order, your ritual is now comfortable, and you see the real benefit of Passage ceremonies. Soon you will be the Elder sitting in Rites of Passage circle ceremonies for others offering wise council.

Always the rattle for a symbolic Death of this age and stage, always a ceremony to bundle the precious gifts recognized and recovered. Dear Soul Sister, for all of the days of this pilgrimage, this is the moment I have looked forward to. I clasp my hands together for allowing me to be your Guide through these Passages. So many old ways need to marry new ways for Passage Rituals to return to the culture, for all of us to grow up and recognize the brilliance in our Souls. Perhaps we will become like mycelium running underground connecting one pod of Elders to another. Congratulations, you have reached a tender time in life, a time when you coalesce with yourself and with the Great Mother. I bow deeply.

I feel like a Dangerous Old Woman and give a nod to my teacher, Clarissa Pinkola Estés[15]. She has offered more than one underground masterpiece for postmodern women to process our lives. I am not exceptional. On this threshold, I accepted her manifesto as my own, I dream in Blood, I dream with the Moon. I am the heart of hope for women and girls, I am only one of an army of awakening women. I feel ferocity for little girls who need opportunities to find themselves, to be chameleons, to survive ordeals, and to cross thresholds offered by Elders.

Elder Encore Threshold

Before anything else, a drumroll. Bow deeply to your initiate Sisters as you all come together and consider the two remaining thresholds. This Elder Threshold is like other thresholds, a culmination of the character building moments, following the red thread of Soul, jousting with Psyche, and enjoying social celebrations with loved ones. Saturn, out in the Cosmos, keeps on asking, have you done all that you came to do? Have you found the courage to claim your legacy? Such is the Nature of accumulating tree rings around your core. Passages need only to be tied with gold and silver threads.

You have caught yourself up, you have grown yourself up. The wide view of all of your Soul meanderings and persistent passions now reveals the truth of change. Initiation happens and then we tell someone. How will you wholeheartedly share the news about reaching this Elder time of your life? Now you flow with an essence of the spiritual river that surrounds you. Life is much less resistance and filled with much more awe.

Perhaps you and your initiate sisters will do your Soul ceremony next to the tree that breathes for you. Once that is complete, the whole community would like the opportunity to embrace and celebrate you. With your Sister initiates, your family, your community, one big potluck may suffice to create awareness that you embrace change. Who doesn't love the idea of a community party for initiating Elders?

Of course, once you arrive here, you are far from finished. Your ritual life is the Queen of everything. She will show you your next steps. So coming to this very special threshold, I will offer this word again, coalesce. Initiation and change require at least one whole year to settle completely into your awareness, into your psyche, and into your language. Practice your rituals and allow this settling. Allow yourself to smile at the two thresholds ahead.

I call this Passage our Elder Encore after a beautiful expression that rose when I was immersed in a training led by Clarissa Pinkola Estés. She encouraged completion, especially during our Elder years. From the audience a woman spoke the word Encore and it spread like a wildfire. Writing *Soul Stories* has begun my Encore, what begins new for yours? This has been an ordeal with a beginning, middle, and an end. As with any Rites of Passage, the community will hold all of my changes up for me to actually see and believe. This is your goal. Your Soul Story needs to be told to make way for the very next opportunity for a Passage ceremony. That next opportunity will come when a woman of the younger generations steps forward and asks you to be a sitting Elder for the Passage she conducts for her daughter. The potential in this is pure evolution in action.

Soon the community who came to your potluck will respond with their needs. Remember what you learned as a busy younger woman, saying no is just as empowering as saying yes. Strengthen our gift economy: Get help with something you need in exchange. Sense the enormity of your Elder role in the culture. All of us want and need initiated Elders, if only to learn about life, to hear stories, and to share awakenings. We bring Rites of Passage as an offering to others of little girls and teen girls. Dear Elder, this is only a conversation, be the leader who opens the conversation.

This is the time to find fearlessness. Our families, yours and mine, need to look up to us for their path, for an image of what completion looks like, feels like, and how being an Elder delivers enormous quantities of joy and love. Create your own way to story this journey. You have worked hard to return to your wholeness. Together we will day by day, story by story, remove the stigma which surrounds the Elder label and return blessings that are only ours to give to our family and community. If you're in need of an infusion of courage, Brené Brown offers *Daring Greatly* and *Imperfections*[7] to clean out the cobwebs of shame that may have lingered throughout adulthood. Both of these books will assist you to locate any lingering hooks over shame, that is the strong energy that holds us back from daring greatly. I say, use Brené's coaching to claim your fearlessness.

If you subscribe to the modern school of thought that the 60s are the new 40s perhaps you just feel too darn good to be called Elder. Yet, your grandchildren celebrate one birthday after another. I do not care if this stage of life lasts 30 or 40 years. Actually I do care. As your reward for all your hard work to keep yourself so young, I hope this stage does last long-long. For your grandchildren, I hope so also. What fun it will be to see their weddings and all their great-babies born.

For your writing pages, because I am such a Coyote, I offer questions to keep you writing. I call this Encore because there is still something inside of you that your Soul pesters you about.

What gifts have you been preparing for and waiting to deliver? What juicy original offering is wanting to be born from your womb? What would spell regret later if you didn't do it now?

This is pay-it-forward time and not just with money. What is your highest calling? How might all of your hard work culminate in one or two fabulous projects that you still need to do? Can you be the driver, the consultant, the mentor? I want to do-do-do, but at this gorgeous age, I have clear boundaries: I write and help out with the childrens' garden at my local rural elementary school. Your family and community need you, but they need you to be happy. Stay in good energetic form, and be present. How is your practice with boundaries?

Whenever you go out on a fabulous jaunt, can you imagine taking a Younger with you, paying expenses in exchange for a Sherpa? Can you imagine being that clear with your grandchild as a traveling companion? The educational benefits alone, to anywhere in the world, expands one's young perception beyond words. Do you recall how your early travels built up a reservoir of confidence and changed your perspective?

When did you learn the secret to moving resistance out of your way? Many women wait their entire lives before they figure out this thing called resistance. One of my doorways to the Divine is through resistance. Resist no more my Dearhearts, call forth your Encore! Resistance is so closely connected to the Divine, it may be colored purple and pushed open. On the other side of your resistance is freedom from stress and ease in solutions.

Brené Brown calls pushing past resistance daring and she suggests summoning courage to face emotional stubbornness or avoidance. Begin this examination of resistance with your flow of energy. Is yours high, medium, or low? What are you resisting? Perhaps it's going to happen anyway and you're wasting energy. There's so much available help; finally, I am learning to see my own resistance, can you see yours? When I realized my blockages had a life of their own, could be colored red for my impatience or green for my not enough-ness, I broke apart resistance. Every time I resist, I wash the subject with a color, and push right through. I am always grateful for the lesson and the release of tension from resisting. Can you see resistance as the doorway to the Divine? Be courageous. Find your resistance about embracing change.

Here, my dear Elders, I want to turn the controls over to you. I said this was going to be a little book, a guide book, a spiritual counselor. What lies ahead is the culminating glory of your life, of our life, yes, together. I trust you have loved your pilgrimage and feel like I have truly guided you.

I am going to repeat just a bit: Light a candle and invite the deepest quiet. From all you have learned, there is ritual, there is a Soul-calling, and there is emotional energy to care for. Allow your quiet to form your own questions. Now that we have come this far together, I cannot know what question remains. I honor my Elder sister Kathleen by offering you this: What question are you holding right now? She changed my life with that challenging question and became one of my twists of fate.

Seek help from any of my suggested authors or find your own. Help abounds. You've come a long way, your ordeals have been enormous, your celebration needs to reflect each one of your Passages.

Place music in your ears, dance the dance of your Soul. Dance in joy for this day, dance the grief-dance for lost Souls, for those who left early, and for those who did not awaken to their Soul's purpose. Dance the dance for the 7 Generations who will be touched by you because you have done this work. Now, celebrate!

Spiritual Elder Threshold

Is this Spiritual Elder our long awaited position on the Spiral? Yes, probably. This is the time to open your sacred bundles and harvest every flake of gold in your life. When you look deeply into all your seasons, you will find the patterns of your life well lived. Your legacy will appear as if by magic. You have been Soul-guided through your life and all of your twists of fate have directed you to this destination.

In how many places did the hand of God or the Divine intervene and come to assist you? When you are able to put your life in proper perspective, you will see that destiny is where you are right now and fateful twists begin to appear highly entertaining. One of my Elder mentors, Joe Meeker, a much loved play specialist and human ecologist,[22] is a man who relishes this position now. He said to me with some glee, "I am finally able to see the patterns of my life." You will finally see the patterns and love this vision as much as he did. Look at any area where you feel resistance. What have you learned about moving through resistance? With the culmination of this life review, a completion is needed. I will not presume to overpower your own creativity.

My Grandmother from my Idaho line, spoke her oral history for the local library gathering pioneer stories. I feel the tears well up when I think of her, and I am so grateful I get to hear her voice. I admit it's a blast from the past because she has been gone decades already. This causes me to think of her lineage, her Mother and her Grandmothers. These are the strong shoulders we stand upon. If there were places with barbs you have released those long ago. Now consider the honoring of you as one of the Ancestors. You could speak your story for your granddaughters and grandsons to hear how your story informs your legacy. Because we live in the digital age, a step beyond the information age, there are so many possibilities for a legacy of your life to be preserved. I love the idea of a campfire and stories told as the stars peek out, but I have that in my genes. Genetic expression is one thing that scientists gave artists, the recognition that a gene may be activated or not. What gene do you have that wants to be expressed?

Know one thing for sure, "Nobody gets out of life alive." Death need not be something that takes us by surprise. Another adventure awaits on the other side of death's doorway. When your time comes, truly comes, do not resist.

You have family and community and circle of women who will honor your ceremonial requests for the final threshold. Women, can we finally learn to do a sweet crossing for one another?

How will you improve on this Rites of Passage process? How will we all prepare ourselves to cross? How do we begin to let go of all the things we love?

Welcome all of the small deaths in your Passage bundles. Do your rituals right through the last 13 Moons. Welcome big D, Death, only when it's your time. Soul knows.

. . .Epilog. . .

I offer the highest praise to every person who holds Rites of Passage in their hearts and offers this sacred ritual to others. This is cultural repair work and through this we are related. I open my arms to all others in this conversation. Leaders teach young and old to look within and use a challenge to mark a new maturity, to shed worn-out skins. Each person is making a difference. I am thrilled that I know many who feel as deeply committed as I to the regeneration of ceremonies in our communities. We work in harmony with Nature to recover our Soul-parts long hidden from view. Our personal recovery will cause a cultural recovery.

Speaking with my humble Elder voice, I place all of us inside the same bubble of forgiving energy and anchor that energy to the ground. These journeys are the most ancient part of our inheritance, but almost all of the stories of our own Elders have been lost to us. We have lived many generations without Soul attention and without Passages. My parents and grandparents and many of yours lived entire lifetimes without these honoring rituals.

We need several generations of stories to rebuild this mythology. Offer forgiveness for anything overlooked and for the places of imperfection where spirit dances most freely; offer forgiveness to me as Guide and to everyone needing this guidance. That is the beginning place: Forgiveness. As the Hawaiian Elders teach, Ho'oponopono, forgive me, I love you.

Live long. Laugh all the way to your grave.

If I taught you to live a ritual life, good!

If I encouraged you to write Memories as a discipline, I feel pleased.

If you demonstrated to yourself that Rites of Passage helped you grow up, brought you to a level of maturity by coalescing your Soul parts, and together we will bring initiation back into the culture, may we say "Ho!" in unison.

I offer my whole heart of love and a deep bow,

Gail Burkett, PhD

Our Soul Stories

We felt invited to this pilgrimage of remembering and sensed the compelling reverence of our nod, like we had been called to enter the shimmering. As women who have grown in our uniqueness, we wanted to share little parts of our journey year. We wanted to feel others' commitment, a sisterhood, a strong thread of connection. Truly companionable yet solitary in our dance with the Cosmos, our pilgrimage to our Soul-selves in Nature brought each one of us into a reciprocal relationship with the Sun and the Moon, with the waters of life, and with our many different personae around the Life Spiral. We are creators of art, of families, of sacred stories, and holy relationships; we are women now initiated through our many Passages.

Julia, Kimberlie, and Sophia pioneered the way around the Life Spiral to their Womanhood Bloom. Their Rites of Passage was deep, joy-filled, and divinely liberating.

Arianna, Judy, Janis, Laura, Kit, Kay, and Gail, initiated Elders now through the Great Earth Mother and her sacred elements, rewove and strengthened the fine filament of our distinctive Souls.

All together, we share our stories in the shimmer of remembering to inspire your *Soul Stories.*

GAIL'S WOMB TIME

One aspect of this design to revisit past time without lingering very long feels trickster-like. I knew my Mother for 50 years, I knew her from inside of her womb too. That's the place I would like to revisit now, down the spirit trail, remembering.

For one long summer month, I laid in the hammock and sat beside the waters of the creek and the lake to return my focus and feel relaxed while imagining my Mother's womb-space. In this deep immersion, I remembered the story waiting for me to be born. In the quiet of each day, sometimes only moments, I discovered messages waiting to come through spirit.

Mother felt welcomed by my California Grandmother, Flora, as daughter-in-law number 8. Think of all those women relations, most of them living in the neighborhood, and all of them with little children. I felt like a spy in the womb as Mother got to know my Aunties.

The part I loved the best was revisiting the huge garden of my grandparents, Harry and Flora. I easily imagined Mother holding me through the thin skin of her belly and watching the bees pollinate the almonds and gather nectar from the boysenberry flowers. She gently waved birds away from the ripening berries. There used to be four acres of serene and welcoming Earth under Flora and Harry's care.

Oh how I loved the sing-song voice of my Father when he came home, often exhausted, all he could do was lay down. He often patted the bed and invited Mother to lie for a few moments and he placed his big hand on her belly, on me. Dad was a new doctor at

San Joaquin General Hospital in Stockton and needed to complete his summer internship after a residency in Family Medicine, both were brutal tests of human capacity. Then, he could set up his own practice.

As the clues arrived, seemingly from nowhere, I realized how well I knew myself through my Mother's reflection. I prepared myself for a metaphoric Birth. As I walked and breathed into this month of immersed remembering, I learned quite interesting things about being carried through a scorching hot California summer. Mother often held my older brother's hand who had turned 3 in April; on her hip my sister Janet who turned 2 late in July before my Birth. Oh dear, I thought over and over, Mother barely had time for me. Two siblings already kept her pretty busy. I know now that 3 more babies came after me, each one diluting Mother's attention again.

Being so closely held in such a big family as Dad's in California was a special miracle for both my Mother and me. So much healing still needed to be done for all who lived through the war, how did they heal? This was definitely a baby boom time in Flora and Harry's lives. Their 8 boys and a girl were all having babies. This was a birth place for me but not a home place.

When the time in November ticked past mid-month, Mother thought perhaps I would be born on her birthday. Instead, I had to be a Scorpio and I absolutely had to be born before dawn. Equal parts of the gene pools of my Mother and Father, my Soul began her meaningful journey on Earth with clarity and intention.

My old Soul had an exalted moment of Birth. Being third born, I was a rather easy delivery. Mother went into serious labor at midnight, checked into the hospital, the delivery doctor was called, but before he could get to the hospital, I was born. My Father caught me at 3:43 a.m. on the last push. As my first clue about Rites of Passage being my true path, being delivered by my Father added a Soul dimension. I was his first obstetrics case in over 3000 babies delivered in his career. Souls always know the circumstances around Birth and take full charge of the very moment of emergence. Since I was born on November 19, I can celebrate my conception day on February 19. This is kind of a fun way to view my gestation. I love that mine was an all seasons in utero experience although Stockton and Modesto barely notice winter.

BIRTH STORY — ANONYMOUS

6/21/14 6 a.m. I am in a room with 4-6 people, like a workshop. We are to create an email. Everyone is in some struggle with this, including me. I go outside to take a break, noticing the beautiful natural world around me. It comes to me that we are all having difficulty, because it means WE ARE CREATING A NEW BEING! I awake in a state of peaceful wonderment.

In Oaxaca, Mexico with a small group to experience the Santo Ninos in Ceremony. I am feeling afraid, wanting to hide from that fact, but clearly quite fearful. I am ambivalent about taking the mushrooms, but also trust the group I am with and am willing to have this experience because it is done in a sacred manner within a container I know is safe. As the medicine is coming on, I notice sparkly lights, geometric shapes and forms coming forward into a light and then receding again. My body feels like it is contorting and I open my eyes to see if in fact it is contorted. I realize I am afraid of being out of control.

I hear the two leaders whispering and I breathe into their prayers. I feel reassured that I am safe. Then I flash on the memory of the illegal Mexican abortion I had when I was 20. There was no emotion when I had this thought, but I also recalled how there was whispering and very low light in the room when the abortion was taking place. Later after the ceremony, when I share with the women about my abortion, the cry of incredible fear and shame comes rolling out. I did not get that it was a baby I was getting rid of – only had fear and concern for my life. In this re-telling, I feel incredible sadness and cry deeply knowing that women all over the world had suffered through such experiences ... and some did not live to tell about it.

I go to sleep that night feeling completely exhausted. Upon waking the energy of this abortion is still with me. I then realize that I am sitting within the passage of conception, moving towards my birth with my birthday coming in 5 days.

Here I am sitting with the awareness that my Mother tried to abort me and I aborted my first pregnancy ... both unwanted babies. What does this mean?

As my fetus self is bathing in the cosmic juices mixed with my mother's own, my dad was molesting my 4 year old sister. It was ramping up in intensity and at times he made my 3 year old brother watch him. I was "holding on" knowing my Mother was angry the abortive herbs that made her bleed did not stop the pregnancy. It's now important and healing for me to know that I do believe that my soul chose to be born into these circumstances. I don't believe that I was being punished or paid back for some wrongdoing in a previous life. What do I experience when I imagine telling out loud my womb story? I experience some shame and feeling exposed. I experience compassion as a woman, for my mother's "predicament." I experience sadness that I was having to absorb all that fear, anger, hatred and being unwanted. I experience the strength of my soul knowing I was to be here no matter what the circumstances.

MIDDLE CHILDHOOD — I WANNA RIDE BY JANIS CLARK

Middle childhood held many terrors. I will remember here the happier moments and recollections, many of which involve HORSES!

I didn't grow up in the country where a girl might find horses. I lived in West Hollywood, one block from the busy intersection of Beverly and La Cienega Boulevards. On that corner was Beverly Park Kiddieland where the movie stars took their kids to ride the child-size Ferris wheel, roller coaster, haunted house, boats, airplanes and such. Best for me was the Merry-Go-Round with all the pretty painted ponies. During the ride, I would daringly climb from horse to horse like a circus performer until I was caught and scolded.

One the other side of La Cienega Blvd. was the Rexall Drug Store with a golden Palomino, a dime a ride. He was my Palomino Pal. Imaginary wind in my eyes, I rode him at least once a week, not quietly either. I yelled Heeyah! whipping him into a gallop.

Down the same block were real pony rides. For fifty cents I could bounce around an enclosed track on a Shetland pony and jiggle my brains loose. I was so hopelessly in love with horses, I imagined my bicycle was a galloping stallion as I jumped curbs. Everyone was looking at me, I imagined. What a good rider, they said.

I earned my Equestrian badge with the Girl Scouts in 1958 after we took riding lessons at Griffith Park. I was a good rider; I could ride any horse. When I was thirty I got my own horse, a beautiful pinto mare, Catalina. This was the first time in my life, I learned, that dreams really do come true.

FIRST BLOOD BY JANIS CLARK

I loved my period. Not at first. Like most young women, when I found blood on my panties, I was horrified. I threw them away. When it happened again, I had to tell Mom; she handed me a belt and a huge wad of Kotex. Nobody told me what to do with the horrid thing when I was ready to discard it, so I flushed it and got in a lot of trouble, living in an apartment.

After that rocky start, things began looking up in the menstruation department. Bleeding was my own personal mystery and I think it actually defined me. I knew I was a woman now; I was included in my Aunties' conversations about women things.

I loved my period, connected to Moon and the tides, slightly crazy, mostly myself, totally connected to everything. My own private mystery, nobody could deny me.

My Grandmother's First Blood was entirely different. When she turned 14 she was married to a man she had never met so as not to risk a pregnancy.

FIRST BLOOD ART BY SOPHIA

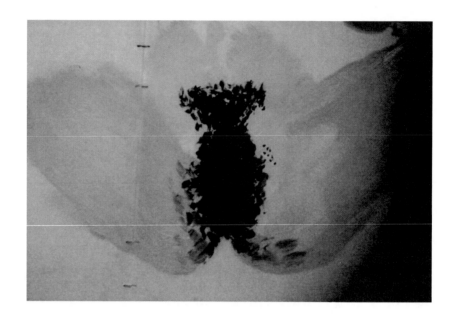

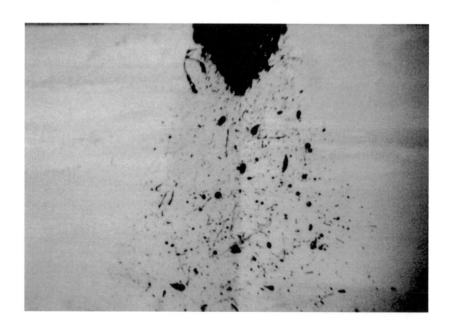

BRIDGE JUMP BY JULIA ZALESAK

My First Blood creative project involves the process to create a Plaster of Paris mask, I ask some of my grad school colleagues to help me. They've been a supportive part of my life for over a year now. To their apartment, I bring over all of the supplies, lay down a sheet to protect the floor, and put pieces of cut straws in my nose so I can breathe through the mask. I lie down and within minutes my mouth is covered so I am only able to answer questions by replying, "mmm hmm," or, "mmm mmm," in different intonations.

It feels good to let go and allow someone to attend to me as I listen to the three other women in the room chat. After a while my mind wanders and I think of the question Gail has suggested we ask as we wear the mask for several nights in a row. I serenely contemplate the question, "What is my purpose?" I am suddenly the center of a torus that is moving swiftly up through me, up and away from my face, out for a bit, then back down toward my feet, and up through me over and over.

Then I'm transported almost exactly twenty years back to the depths of the Ohio Missouri Channel off the coast of Ohio Key, Florida, in the middle of the night. I've just turned sixteen and I've plunged deeper into the pitch black, shark filled waters than I'd anticipated. I'm swimming straight up as quickly as I can toward the surface to gasp for air.

My lungs are burning for the next breath of air that I'm not sure if I will ever take.

There is something timeless and comforting about the memory of that moment even though the inhalation of my next breath was uncertain. The pitch dark expanse of the ocean felt like an enveloping, supportive presence. That mysterious presence lured me in. I'm moved every time I think of it.

How did I end up in such a precarious situation you may be asking? Well I will tell you. First I need to back up a few years.

When I was twelve, my family started spending every winter break at the same campground in the Florida Keys. There were a good number of families that followed the same tradition. As a result, the year I turned fourteen, I became friends with a group of young people who were all about the same age as me.

We developed into a pretty intimate community of friends. We explored the island or played games all day and then had bonfires and stargazed at night. Someone might bring an instrument like a guitar or a reed flute and we'd sing. Sometimes we contemplated mysteries out loud and shared stories all night long. We spent so much time together that we barely separated to eat meals with our families or to sleep. New people were always welcome and so were their stories.

We had really deep conversations compared to the ones I had with my peers at school. We would have fire circles where we would share with each other, parts of ourselves, undiscovered by our friends at school. I think this is because we could tell we all appreciated each other for who we truly were. We also didn't have anything to lose by sharing parts of ourselves that weren't consistent with what our peer groups would have us say or do. We agreed that we probably wouldn't be friends if we went to the same school because we belonged to different crowds. However, we also agreed that we were grateful to have the amazing conversations and connections that we did, even if it was just two weeks a year.

My fifth winter break there, I was standing with a friend and looking over the fishing bridge into that gorgeous deep turquoise water in the middle of the day. I was overcome by this strong longing to find a way to just BE in that mysterious magnificence. I mentioned this to my friend and she agreed. Somehow that turned into a whole group of about ten of us walking down the bridge in the middle of that night to where the water was deep enough to jump in. Anticipation, fear, and excitement were in the air. We all jumped in one at a time, most of us hesitating a bit before jumping.

I remember going second. It was pretty dark since the island was a campground and there weren't any city lights. The bridge was high enough that when I hit the water I went so far down that it took quite a while to get back to the surface of the water. There was something about that seemingly long swim back to the surface in the pitch dark that I can't quite articulate but it left a lasting impression on me. When we all got back to shore, we were the happiest most excited group of teenagers ever. We immediately changed into dry clothes and met up on the other side of the island to sit around a fire and share our personal stories of the bridge jumping. Those deeper than normal experiences for two weeks each year did something BIG for my soul and added significant richness to my life.

Did we feel the need to self-initiate in the absence of elders who could facilitate for us? What does this memory mean for me? What does the torus have to do with any of it?

FIRST FLIGHT — SPIRITUAL JOURNEY BY JANIS CLARK

When I was a little girl, I loved the Spirit world. It seemed to me to exist just the other side of the door.

Our Catholic life was filled with ritual: Mass every Sunday; Easter week with the Stations of the Cross; Holy Days of Obligation (of which there were many) and Christmas. The sanctity of these holy devotions were followed by huge dinners at Grandma and Grandpa's house, the whole family sitting around the big table, plates of food presented one after the other and lots of laughter.

After my divorce I was cut loose from the Catholic Church and the spiritual world I had grown up with. I was left with a vacuum to fill.

For no apparent reason, while in a head shop one afternoon, I picked up The I Ching or Book of Changes with a foreword by C.G. Jung. The I Ching is considered to predate recorded history. Using a system of hexagrams as the exponent of the moment in which they were cast, the I Ching was a common source for both Taoist and Confucian thought. I had never heard of it.

The underlying idea of the I Ching is change. Confucius said, standing by a river: "Everything flows on and on like this river, without pause, day and night." Jung explains, "This is the eternal law at work in all change. This law is the Tao of Lao-tse. Change is not meaningless…but subject to universal law."

I learned to throw the coins and read the hexagrams, in the beginning not so much for divination, but for help. To my surprise, I was able to read for myself and for others the meaning of the symbols, which in turn explained and predicted events. Thus began my new spiritual journey, exchanging one ancient philosophy for another, a First Flight into a new spiritual journey.

THE ABYSS By Kimberlie Gridley

For ages I skirted the abyss.
At times stopping to peer over the edge,
Movement within, caught my sight
To hear my name called from the depths.

I would move on, away from the chasm
To the safety of the wide plain,
Or so it would seem.

Lightning strike or fierce attack,
I start running.
Before long, the abyss is upon me,
I nearly slip off the edge,
Skid to a halt just in time.

Below me is a bottomless indigo
Visions of future and past spiral in deadly,
Or so it would seem,
Whirlpools.

"Do you hear them?"
"Who?"
"I don't know. But do you hear them?"
I would ask.
"I hear nothing."
The deafening reply.

"Can you see them?"
"Who?"

156

"Them."
I would plead.
"I see no one."

Whatever you think you hear,
Whomever you think you see,
Is unreal.
Your imagination, run away.

The darkness tempting you to damnation.
Nothing good can come from below.
The underworld.
Hell,
Calling you to perform unthinkable evil deeds?

No!
Kindness,
Joy,
Laughter,
Understanding!?

You are mistaken child.
Turn away.
And so I did.

Back to the plain,
The wide open lonely plain.
Full of predators, drought.
I moved closer to the abyss.
Just a look.
A listen.

I won't jump
Into the unknown.

Back and forth
Between worlds
Under the cover of darkness
The veil of sleep.

When vision becomes reality
I move away
Got too close.
The barometer of safety.

Walking above the water,
One day,
I cross your path.
I know you,
Though we have never met.
The abyss must be nearby
I think to myself.
But I know now
I will not jump.
I am in control.

Lost in conversation
We become.
One.

We are upon it now.
The abyss
I look in and say.

158

"Can you hear?
Do you see?"

"Take my hand"
You reply.
Then you leap.
We are in free fall now.
I can no longer see your face.
It is getting so dark
Feeling fingers interlaced.

Despite the descent
Faces turn upward
Away from the darkness
that awaits.

The light
From above
is blinding at first
Deeper and deeper
We fall.

The light begins to dim.
The visions fly past and future
Indistinguishable
One
From Another

I can hear the voices in my head
Feel their breath on my face.
Languages unknown

Forgotten in time.

So much to learn
Falling so fast.
One quick squeeze and
I know you are still there.

Why?
Did you jump?
Are we here?
Together.

A memory
Or so it would seem.

Conscious of earth
Beneath my feet.

I turn to you
You look away
I see you
Naked to the bone

I look away
I feel your stare
Look down
Naked to the bone
You look away.

What now?
Let go
And climb!

I begin this long ascent.
The fear of falling
Barely a memory
Now

Naked to the bone
I explore
My surroundings
Myself
The bone

Like rings on a tree
Layers of onion
Digging down
Boring
All the way
Into marrow

Faintly
I make out your shape
Huddled
Chipping away
At bone

Crawling along
on earth
the floor of the abyss

I search until I find
The wall
No rope
I start
The climb

Alone?
Yes.
and No.

I hear a voice beside me
In the dark
¡Hola!

There you are again
I smile
And get back to work.

Hands of the Elder

Womanhood Bloom - Laura

First flight and emancipation ended for me hard at 29 years old. I had gone to college, Europe, moved to New York City, fallen in love, hard, twice and more travel, more Europe, South America several times. I had a career, I had the best mentors. And then I was Coyote in Road Runnner – Beep beep – BAM, off the edge of the cliff and nothing under me...

I looked at my life and it had none of the elements I wanted, earth, 4-leggeds, family or home. These things weren't even on the horizon. I got 2 cats from Chinatown, kicked out my depressed boyfriend and I felt sad, tired and broken hearted. I wished for a disease that was just bad enough that if I changed my whole life and took care of myself I'd beat it. I must have said that out loud because at some point I realized I didn't need a disease I just had to take care of self. So I began that process.

I spent 6 months planning; I travelled to Seattle and to New Mexico, then decided to move to Montana, site unseen and absolutely no connections and no job. It didn't seem rash, it seemed passionate and feeling based. It felt right and I needed to feel right.

Before leaving NYC I did my leaving ritual of sorting through photos and organizing albums, I felt the calling for more ceremony, we had god-speed parties and good-bye parties. I found some great occult book stores and created my own ritual. I put valued pieces of self in a tiny silver capsule and sealed it with wax, I climbed up my fire escape, past my neighbors living rooms to my rooftop. I lit candles and bared my breast. I softly chanted my intentions, 13 times, getting louder and louder until I screamed them at the top of my lungs. My arms open. Power surged through my archetypical cry. I blew out my candle, put my shirt on and glanced at the buildings looming over my lowly rooftop. No one shouted back.

I packed up my ferral kitties and said good-bye to NYC and my friends. I bravely left for the mountains.

The journey was a mix of fear and excitement. I relied on my spirit animal the she-wolf who was introduced to me by a Shaman in New York. The first winter was hard. I made one friend. I spent time alone. I skied and I found my soul mate in a big, beautiful dog from the shelter, Paris Gibson. I healed. I learned to build motorcycles and engines, I hiked and mountain biked with my P-dog.

At night I would wake up, not knowing were I was but knowing I hadn't found home yet. It was an eerie out of my body-experience, as if my old soul was poking my present life and saying "You're not home yet, keep moving."

I met a man that would be the father of my children. We made a family, married, had dogs, horses kids and our family grew. We settled, bought a ranch, worked 3 jobs plus the job of raising 2 babies. By the time I hit my next passage into deepening womanhood I had 4 children (not all from my womb) 12 horses, 6 dogs and was too busy juggling all the balls, paying all the bills to care for myself and they all fell down but thats another passage/growth story...

ONE SEVEN YEAR INITIATION BY GAIL BURKETT

Nearly every day I am out in the woods with my dog practicing what Thich Nhat Hanh teaches, walking meditation. I carry my camera to capture the daily wonders, but mostly I empty my tired old mind out on the trail. Great Mother Earth can handle anything I need to release or transform. Over the years I have found that in such emptiness, usually one good idea squeezes its way in, kind of knocking and wondering, are you feeling receptive?

Through this pilgrimage of remembering, I made this connection. This writing and eldering journey began in 1995 when my walking practice first began. I remember the inspiration about redesigning my life had come through a little tiny seed thought: every single one of those 3 or 4 trillion cells that make me, me, will be completely remade new in only seven years. At age 44, I knew that was a long time and a short time, but I was mesmerized by the very thought of a make-over, an over-haul, a totally new me. I wanted no carry forward from my former life. Erasing history was not possible; my mind has memory for a reason, but I needed to release the shame I felt for wasting my youthful energy as a corporate cog.

That was the first time I peeled the metaphoric onion to process my bundle of trauma and the pain of living. Now I know age 44 is not that old actually, but it felt like a lifetime and my former years were especially burdened. This conscious and thoughtful transformation was a good idea then and is still a good idea for anyone who wants to avoid a mid-life spiritual emergency. From inside the protective umbrella of graduate school, year by year, my worldview about initiation and transformation grew. Over these past twenty years, I have developed a body of work originating in deep studies of indigenous Rites of Passage ceremonies and building something new. An idea gift came on one of my walks—marry those old ways with new ways and use a life spiral, the way the Earth creates seasons. I call this Birth to Death journey, *Nine Passages*, but it took a long time to see the whole.

Today, in an empty mind state, I simply watched ice form over the beaver dam and remembered my first Passage ceremony into Deepening Womanhood. I lived in a converted 1940's dining car that had been dragged up the mountain to be a mess hall for loggers. For 50 years that boxcar had rested on a flat place nestled in lodge pole and ponderosa pines at 8000' before Sierra and I moved in. As rustic as it gets, I dearly love the memory of living there. On Halloween 1995, I woke to two feet of new snow and the next day two more feet fell. I was snowed in and suddenly locked inside a catalyst of change like I had never experienced.

Sierra's low growl woke me around 3:30 a.m. Soft moonlight reflected on the snow and lit up the procession of elk following one another. I wrapped one arm around my fiercely protective dog to quiet my own excitement and invite her to watch the parade. At that time of the morning, just before the minute of my Birth, I thought of the labor pains that brought me forth into the world. As I counted the elk moving slowly through the deep snow past my bedroom window, I thought of my life, patterns and gifts, I thought of the future unfolding as a doctoral candidate. I could make up for lost time, it wasn't too late to start over; the best of my life had to be ahead.

What would I study? Suddenly opportunity, possibility, and my own entelechy seemed pressing. "Present moment," I said returning my attention to the elk, now numbering more than 30. Feeling the treasure of this wonder unfolding, tears fell down my cheeks. I had to wipe my nose on my pillowcase. Soon the bull elk showed up and I realized I had been watching and counting cows and calves and the bulls brought up the rear. My count had reached into the 70s before the massive Elder bull with antlers touching his tail stopped before the picture window and turned his head. While our eyes were locked, the question I was holding was instantly answered. When he turned back to the procession, he had stood still long enough to be the last remaining visible elk. He quickened his pace and disappeared into the trees.

The penetrating eyes of the oldest elk echoed his Elder status. Something else happened while I stoked the fire, an apparition of my Grandfather appeared. He seemed to help me load kindling and strike the match. I turned to see his brother, Uncle Fred, and my Grandmother too. They were filmy, not in their bodies, exactly, but they had a message. I sat on the little step beside my potbelly stove with all thoughts suspended and waited. Their parents appeared behind them, even more translucent, but quite clearly, seven apparitions crowded around my tiny stove. To this day, I laugh at the next thing I did. I said, "Could I offer you coffee and oatmeal?"

They all seemed to nod and I got busy. They were still there when I returned to the stove with my offerings, "This will take a few minutes." But I had realized it was All Souls' Day, this is the one day of the year when I am supposed to suspend beliefs and welcome my Ancestors to a hearty meal. With tears brimming my eyelids again, Gammie Board shushed me and I said, "Welcome! Welcome!" and sat quietly waiting.

Their communication was not exactly audible, I do not actually remember a sound. Without using words, they had plenty to tell me. I received a download while we waited for oatmeal to heat and cook. Soon the coffee began to smell wonderful all through my boxcar home. I dished up eight little bowls of oatmeal and felt so blessed to have the right number of bowls. I opened a new can of condensed milk hoping it would be enough and sat quietly again.

My Great Grandmother Emily was the spokesperson. I had never met her and barely knew her as my relation except for a photo that had hung in my grandparents' house. She had remembered seeing elk on the plains on the trip over from England but there were none in the mountains of Idaho. Her sons chimed in and said, "Not until 1942 when they were off loaded from the train cars."

In my life since that day I have come to believe everything from the world of spirits is generous and offered for our evolution. My Ancestors came in my waking dream for just an hour and have not appeared again, they have not needed to employ such drama for me to know of their presence. They delivered many gifts in that hour, but the greatest was the catalyst of change. I was welcomed to the second half of my life as they offered their blessings for the first half. Until I received their blessing, I had a low opinion of my life experience and that all changed.

I have not shared this story often, but today I recognize that I was offered as fine an initiation as I have ever imagined and opened every door. My Rites of Passage into the Deepening Womanhood stage of my life was cellular and transformative.

DEEPENING WOMANHOOD BY JANIS CLARK

Something
Must be gained
From all this Sorrow,
A costly barter
To be made.
We come away
Shaking heads, and
Wondering why?
Some of us
Profess belief
In Cosmic answers
And I admit a comfort in
"It was meant to be."
Let us bless
Even Sorrow;
For having shed our skin
Have we not added
Yet another rattle,
Grown bigger
by Sorrow's feeding?

ELDER ENCORE — GRANDMOTHERS BY JANIS CLARK

As I have thought about my own life, I have also thought about my Ancestors:

Great great grandmother Teresa, sailed from Italy in 1870 with her husband, Gianbattista, and four young children, to arrive in New York at age 41. Two years later, she died in a Manhattan tenement apartment where three other families lived. The cause of death was peritonitis and metritis purpereal (inflammation of the uterus). I wonder if she was pregnant. She is buried in a pauper's grave in Calvary Cemetery, Queens, NY.

Grandma Filomena, was married at 14 to a man she had never met. Filomena's brother Tony had gotten his girlfriend pregnant and great grandma Rosa wasn't taking any chances. Grandma Filomena had her first child when she was 16. She was a good mother, but she had wanted to go to high school. She died at 84 in her sleep after enjoying an independent life for twenty-one years, airline tickets on the table.

Grandma Lena always lied about her age. When we had her 90th birthday party, she was actually 91, but we didn't know that until I began family research. Grandma Lena finished eighth grade, but worked cleaning copper pots for Mrs. Wright's silver polish company and lighting the shop lamps when she was eight years old. She died peacefully at 93, handing Dad her hearing aids, "I don't think I need these; I'm going to die now." Lena's father Andrea died at thirty-three of tuberculosis when she was only two and Lena's mother, Antonia, sold apples, chestnuts and popcorn on the streets of Manhattan before she moved the family to Keene, NH where she opened her own confection shop. Antonia supported five children by herself; she didn't speak English. She died at 56.

Grandpa Carmine, Joseph and Gaetana came to America in 1891; Gaetana was pregnant on the boat. Carmine was four years old when they left Naples. Gaetana had seven more children in ten years and died at forty-four years old.

My mother Rita and father Joseph were married 56 years. Dad has been gone sixteen years now and Mom lives very well on her own at age 94, still driving and getting around.

I wonder what each of those women whose chromosomes are part of me thought about their lives. What were their expectations? Where was their happiness? How deep was their despair?

Donne della mia famiglia, ti amo tutti. Ladies of my family, I love you all.

ENTERING ELDERHOOD — ANONYMOUS

Completing my passage of Deepening Womanhood, I stand ready to embrace the Elder. This is my time of life. I am ripening with such excitement. Since retiring, my approach to Eldering has been reading, listening, observing and praying for guidance for about two years now. Two days before reaching this passage, I get asked to join an Elders' Council that will create programming for a Women's Retreat, developing and growing other women into their Elder seat for the community. I say YES!!

While attending a two day retreat with this Elders' Council, we are led into a circle of sacred movement. We are to flow into the center, eyes closed, and move our body authentically, while being witnessed by those in the outer circle with eyes open. We move in and out of the center as our bodies tell us to do so. While witnessing, I see a woman on all four's, her hands searching the floor. She finally connects with the feet of someone witnessing her movement. I weep in gratitude for this moment, and my body pulls me into the center to connect with this touch. I soon surrender to this longing and lay sobbing on the floor in complete gratitude for the safety of this moment, to hold her feet and to be touched and held in return.

Others join in the center asking permission to hold and carress me. I feel my pain and THE PAIN of all older women who have accumulated longing for this nurturing cacoon of touch that is without expectations of any kind. This is my initiation ceremony into becoming an Elder.

After the initial excitement of saying YES to join this circle of women agreeing to work our way through these passages on the

Life Spiral, I feel the contraction; back into doubt, questioning, with some judgment ... What else could possibly be revealed about these points in my life that I haven't already explored? I spent 38 years as a child and family therapist, and doing my own therapy along the way. There is the longing that I am present to, but it feels more like longing for my tribal sisters to enter into this journey with me regardless of where it takes me. The next morning I awake with this thought ... "You're not going through this to heal old wounds. This will be a process of initiating myself as an Elder through each of these passages so that I will know what experiences and wisdom I can best offer to my Community."

GAIL'S PILGRIMAGE THROUGH SOUL STORIES

A teaching from long ago has echoed all through my *Soul Stories* journey to celebrate my thresholds of change: Clarissa Pinkola Estés offered a story of descansos, Spanish for the places of rest. Along roadsides, memorials of remembrance mark a passing, a death of something. All of my yesterdays have now been placed in little descansos all along my beach.

For my Birth threshold and all that came after, I transformed a Wheel of Life into a Life Spiral. I especially love the symbols that showed up in the three threads of stone—Divine Masculine and Divine Feminine becomes whole at Birth when my Soul flies in from the stars.

175

For the 30 days the Sun moved through the sign of Leo, I celebrated the innocence and stories of my little self, playful and naïvely blissful. Before I was 8, I was unwounded and happy to learn to walk and talk, to read and write and alternately visit grandparents in central Idaho and central California. The age of responsibility and its Middle Child threshold delivered my first heart wound and my first physical wounds. I remembered all the days in the best way I could, adding a stone or two every day to a little descanso on the island between the split creeks.

To celebrate the bittersweet chaos of my adolescence, for First Blood I made order out of my heart rock collection as my homage, the descanso marker for early and middle adolescence. In the midst of the deepest feeling of grief, and sinking into the stark contrast between my innocence and chaos, I felt joy with each beautiful heart stone that helped me see the heroine of my 14 and 15 year old self. What a remembrance for my teenage self. Somehow I made heart out of the twist of teenage hormones and brain chemistry cocktail while my tender young girl self learned about death and tragedy and the unfairness of life. When I see this on the beach I know she is me.

I felt nothing but relief and excitement when First Flight came. I felt honored to step out entirely on my own and look after my needs. My memories came pouring forth, I felt collegiate during that first summer and autumn. My first winter out of the home nest I found a way to take night classes so I could ski at Alta every single day. Then life found its way with me, what goes up cannot stay up, so I came all the way down to the ground. The lessons of my 20s did not have to be repeated, thank goodness, and before I turned 30, I twirled at the threshold of my Womanhood Bloom, on the streets of New York City. I was changed because Death had visited again, and again, and again.

Those New York years deserved a little desconso, I thought. My place of rest marker for Womanhood Bloom grew into an arrow of sorts because I was such a warrior and felt so Divinely Masculine as I clung to the corporate ladder. I have come to understand my destiny is one with Death because I have confronted Death in so many ways. The memories of my 30s are sweetly distilled now, nothing like the terror and thousand little deaths I felt throughout that decade.

The ground became too frozen to play with stones, they were one with the Earth through my remembrance of Deepening Womanhood. I am unable to understand all there is in the unseen world, yet I make sense of the gift that Grouse Creek delivered to me. I felt celebratory relief for crossing the Deepening Womanhood threshold and remembering my bold awakening. Just two days after I crossed that threshold on Winter Solstice to examine my life from 52 to 64, a little stone Goddess appeared to help me through the memories, joyful and more awake with each passing day.

I could hardly refuse her company. SHE is a stone in the shape of a beautiful Goddess. I couldn't help but notice that. She beached like a whale and I stood her upright. Feeling profound respect for the spirit inside of her, I whispered thanks and welcomed her home. I laughed out loud because I have always known that stones float and that is how she came to be with me. She easily weighs 70 pounds but did not float away again. Even though waters hit flood stage three times she stayed, and stayed, and stayed through all the days of deep cold in our northern winter. Maybe her trials represented my trials. I encouraged her to settle in a place above the flood line and she rested uneasy there until I gave her a proper position. Through the next two Sun signs she demonstrated how much she wanted to be with me; I went to the waters to visit her every day.

After twenty years of offering Rites of Passages for so many others I speak a symbolic language unique to me. This is how spirituality comes to all of us, I think, our days are spiced with signs and symbols that we interpret. In my own private Rites of Passage and my Elder threshold, I made my little Earth Goddess comfortable, above the flood waters. I have asked her to be my marker for all the days that have gone before. Descanso lives in her as a place of rest.

Why do I care about Rites of Passage? I live in awe of the vision of uplifting Elders to an honored and initiated place: This is my purpose. Our search for self, Soul, purpose, or vision is big work at any age. I feel the deep bond of sorrow when I hear of any woman who has not located her Soul's purpose. Passage rituals remind us of the Genius and purpose within our Soul and will help our culture grow up. This sorrow I feel over unrealized gifts or purpose connects to my Soul mission to offer women ways to remember and complete their precious transformations. The ritual for each Passage claims the change locked inside those moments to call forth illumination and transformation. It's never too late to reclaim your purpose.

I wrote *Soul Stories* to put the mystery of searching in perspective. By pulling together all the pieces of your development, you will gain a truthful understanding of your evolutionary timeline and visualize patterns that may suggest next steps in your spiritual development. When you complete this pilgrimage and locate forgotten seeds of your Soul, a trajectory will align with the roots of your evolution and nourish you.

Ours is the struggle to become fully human. I have identified Nine Passages which are universal to all women. *Soul Stories* will bring those Passages up for you, make them personal, and guide you through each one to complete your transformation. Change is deeply magical and beautiful. Within the truth of our natural history—change is all there is. To become fully human means embracing metamorphosis and completing each transformation. All stages of your development, every event will be rewrapped to restore your wholeness.

A crescendo of development has pushed you to a transformative edge more than once. I want to help you recognize those precious moments when your spiritual aspects—mind, body, breath, and Soul—reached the edge.

You traveled into many growth cocoons in development; you emerged as a butterfly, but were you stopped? Did you receive a warm welcome from your family and tell your ordeal story to receive the blessings of belonging from your community? Many butterflies get lost in the wilderness. Without ritual to honor the many trials, some pains of life remain as unhealed wounds that surface and cycle through present day stories causing more havoc.

Since this Rites of Passage conversation has recently returned to the culture, stories will soon emerge about other life Passages and ceremonial rituals for growth will wrap around motherhood, marriage, anniversaries, divorce, and every other personal growth marker. All of our beautiful, inevitable choices are life-changing blessings, ironies, and twists of fate. Our stories need to safely be received and held because we are storytellers. Telling the story completes the Passage.

The Story Began with 3Beauties

I found my old self bunking with two delightful beauties. They were half my age but ringing my faint little memory bell, supple and sensuous in ways I wanted to remember. A third beauty slept across the hall of our bunkhouse. How we got together is one of the great mysteries of chemistry, we were drawn together. The occasion was a gift really, a conversation called *Initiation* where Michael Meade[6] called us into a space and began to tell us stories. He offered mythos and songs from the Ancestors that healed our psyches. Michael was in rare form and each time a story was told or a song was sung, our very Souls cracked open a little bit more.

Curiously immersed, our conversations and attentions focused on initiation. Every moment felt synchronistic because my life work revolves around Rites of Passage. One new friend asked, "What are you painting, what is that thing?" I love the inspiration of altered mind space. When Michael Meade told the story of Poder, I sat on the back row listening to locate his skill-set, how did he lead us into story that caused our brains to rapid fire? I dipped a paint-brush into my tea and then into a portable water color set. Dip, paint, listen-listen. Also listening to my inner voice, I found myself in grief over this story of Poder, a baby boy born with observable gifts. I felt a longing that we could all know our gifts in such an easy manner. The tentacles of Poder's story attached to thoughts of every one of my relations, as well as myself. I realized by design, initiations "revealed one's gifts to oneself" in Meade's words, mag-ical words![6]

Dip, draw. Soon I had painted a Life Spiral that represented the biological Passages from Birth to Death. These are universal Passages because all women experience them and in the same order: Birth, Middle Childhood, First Blood, First Flight, Womanhood Bloom, Deepening Womanhood, Elder Encore, Spiritual Elder and Death. My Spiral placed Death in the middle because leaving each stage of life is a little death of that stage. Also, Death travels with each one of us, all through life. After a little human enters Middle Childhood about eight, nine, or ten years old, individuation takes a journey through us, through our bodies and our psyches. Every person's story and every person's gift-set is different from everyone else's.

FIVE THRESHOLDS FOR 3BEAUTIES

Step back in time to the Autumnal Equinox of 2013. At the very end of a workshop about ritual and initiation, a room full of light hearted Souls swung open the French doors and breathed the rarified air. We sang one more song, we wanted one more hug, and in truth we had received almost too much to think about. Over four days, transformation had planted herself in the mind of our hearts.

I felt the nudge of courage push me to the edge of my edge. After sharing intimate stories for what seemed an altered length of time, I looked three beautiful young women directly in the eye and asked, "Would you like me to guide you through Rites of Passage?" The moment was just a moment. We bowed and bowed again and bowed all together. In such a reverent posture our hearts were engaged and we said yes in unison.

Camped in a scout's stronghold west of Seattle for this long weekend, gently held in tall pines and balmy weather, we quickly moved deeply into ourselves and deeply into ritual with mythologist Michael Meade as he wrapped his brilliance around a topic mostly out of our culture—initiation.[6] He cared for our Souls in ways that caused cracks in our armor. Lacking a cultural concept for initiated women or any true container for holding a lengthy personal ceremony, four of us began to imagine how to create such a bridge.

I had prepared myself for fifteen years; any doubt I felt dissolved into their obvious need and desire. These women, all women, needed a chance to meet themselves, their Souls, and their Genius. I could only use forgiveness to overcome my own audacity because I was not prepared for the exhilaration of my daring question. I asked for forgiveness because the initiation I offered these 3Beauties did not exist. It has been far too long out of the culture. I needed help from the Ancestors to create something new out of something old, imagined, and relevant.

We all gathered our forces from the Moon and the Sun, from

the Cosmos herself to call forth five Passage thresholds. From inside of their Mother's womb the first threshold appeared slow as cold molasses and the others followed in proper cosmic order. I hold truth telling and authenticity up with personal power, and used the magic of encouragement for each woman's story to emerge from deep within their personal inspiration. To move them forward along their personal timelines we ran a closed and intimate women's sharing circle through our cyberspace connections and marked a new Passage each month.

This women's way of initiation appeared through illumination from the far side, from intuition. I walked through three long seasons—through the glory of fall, the deep snow of winter, and into the waking of springtime with the fierce and delicate spirits of these three women. The prayers during those walks invoked the Grandmothers' spirits and I was well enough guided to upright myself and be the guide they needed day by day and week by week.

I told them, your way of catching-up with a lifetime of initiations begins with the story already running in your family when the embryo of you swam in the oceanic womb of your birth Mother. To begin a womanhood initiation in the midst of our cultural lack, we feel it is both urgent and proper to begin at Birth.

For these three women, I held firm to my commitment and encircled their liminal space with powerful prayers and received help far beyond my capacity. The insights from my prayers were regularly uploaded through the marvelous web of the cyber-spider as the Sun moved through the zodiac. What started on Fall Equinox, ran beyond Spring Equinox without stopping. A new threshold appeared at each progressive astrological sign. By Winter Solstice they crossed the threshold for leaving home, for their First Flight. They each found far more to dwell on, so I asked them to focus on Soul-seeds, parts of themselves left behind that would serve them today.

I sent life stage descriptions and initiation stories for each threshold. Hoping a unique sacred space was created in the deep silence of Nature, each woman gave new life to her old stories. Michael Meade told us and we agree, living in the now is most enjoyable, but our past is always with us. For one month in each stage of life, *remembering* was elevated to a ritual place. Each beautiful woman stepped into ritual and across thresholds, witnessed only by the natural world.

Perhaps women's truest ally is the Moon and we used the dark New Moon and the bright Full Moon for gathering the medicine of the past ages. In watching the Moon carefully, in her reflection, they learned so much about their bodies' natural rhythms. We are neophytes in our relationship with Grandmother Moon, but we feel this is one energy to know better.

The Soul journey of these 3Beauties found key memories to bundle for each of their vitally human stages of being: Birth, Middle Childhood, First Blood, First Flight, and Womanhood Bloom. They did the work, I held sweetly and firmly to the belief that Soul-seeds of initiation would unlock their inherent Genius. That Soul-self, inner Genius, always steps forward under the protection of immersion and intention.

. . .

CLOSING CEREMONY

Calling on their personal power and intuitive design, they asked for a completion ceremony to close their initiation portal just before the new Moon of May. We met at Soap Lake, half way from each home base. Through the dark of the Moon, in sacred ceremony, five of us, 3 Elders and 2 initiates gathered to close the portal we so carefully opened when we bowed. The woman across the ocean came in-absentia and in spirit. I offered a recording of her story.

Quite wonderful woman-stories aligned with time to re-birth the oral tradition of folk psychology and bring new life to initiation. For eight months I had summoned dream time and the altered space directly out of my deep sleep to call forth my Elder-self. Each initiate brought a special gift to our gathering, her Mentor, a beloved Elder and wise advisor, who helped hold her from the beginning. We made time for stories, initiation stories and get acquainted stories to nourish our Souls.

After we laid a careful altar, lit the candles and drummed and danced to raise our energy, I launched beyond the check-in and the Thanksgiving Address into the storytelling. The two initiates easily chose first and second position and began. We heard a grand version of the Thanksgiving Address over lunch and a good little check-in after breakfast the second morning. We designated twenty-four hours as our time to wrap our bundles and close the sacred portal of initiation.

The vision of their long ritual spreads out over cosmic time, moving with the Sun and the Moon; these ancient guides of the Cosmos helped us penetrate the deep space of memory. What started with those long, honoring bows, and traveled with the Cosmos, ended with three whole stories of these women's lives. It feels miraculous to hold story within story, how ritual wraps a life story into a bundle with new meaning. In cosmic time, sunrise and moonrise renewed each woman's spirit as her life-view expanded at each threshold. Memories unfold to reveal the essence of Soul-story and a transformation suited to these times. Now the ears in my heart hold these stories as a sacred gift, forever.

We held the essential energy of transformation with great care. One woman completed her divorce and cautiously fell into a new love, one completed graduate school and a vision quest, and one woman quit a career of a dozen years and cast herself into free fall with trust as her Soul ally. They shed these skins as they danced across five thresholds with grace and with tears.

Each woman transformed herself using the Spiral of Life to honor each Passage and awaken her Soul. Even before the *year after initiation* ended, all three women looked back to see a uniquely different persona who emerged. Each one worked through her story, diving deep into her inner mine to harvest the nuggets of her life. Each woman grieved, prayed, and gathered her bundle of Soulseeds. Each woman slept with her Genius and her awakened Soul through dreamtime, rising with her fire-center to claim wholeness. My greatest life privilege accepts this role to delicately hold such rejuvenating stories of a whole life.

WHAT IS AN ELDER? BY REV. ARIANNA HUSBAND

According to Clarissa Pinkola Estes, it is not an 'age' in years … it's a continual learning journey. An Elder becomes a carrier of accumulated life experience and wisdom.

An Elder slows things down … watches, observes, deeply listens … asks questions to encourage and lead individuals or groups toward their own knowing.

An Elder forms a bridge to the future, by carrying life experience and memories of times past and holding hands with the creative, insightful youth, bringing forth vision in the present.

Elders pray for the people and hold them in their heart, their work done mostly invisibly. Elders affirm individuals, watch for and affirm their gifts. Elders attend and participate in initiations and Rites of Passage conducted by the mature adult/teachers/young Elders of community for the youth and adults of all stages.

The Elders bless at every opportunity: with feathers, sacred herbs, water/salt, song, words, loving gaze, laying on of hands. Elders speak blessings like these to the ones younger than ourselves: "I love that you here; I'm glad for you in the world; I am proud of you; you are so loveable; you are precious to all of us; I love you."

In the same way, Elders who now walk in the world without parents or mentors, with no one to bless them, need and are nourished by the blessings from those younger who say, "I am so glad you are alive. You matter on this earth; don't die," even though it scares us a little bit to hear.

Elders tend to arising grief and bring the Ancestor and Spirit connection in all things and encounters; they carry life experience manifested as wisdom in mysterious ways that are not really able to be described in a "bio." Perhaps one has lived a life, of say 60+ years, and is sitting with an individual or group. A question arises, or something is happening that sparks a memory in the Elder, which then brings forth a story. Spirit has moved the story to come forth, not remembered until now, to nourish the people or situation. We can't even plan for these moments. We need to walk in humble trust and willingness to be of service, and as much as possible be a hollow bone for Spirit to bring forth the nourishment that is needed at the right moment.

Sobonfu Somé and Michael Meade say that the Elders bring the water to the ceremony; they provide the nourishing waters of life for the people and creation. Paul Raphael's Odawa people say the women bring the water for nourishing new life; they carry the birthing and nourishing waters of life.

Michael Meade shares that when a societal body or culture forgets its Elders, then Elders do not know their value. When an Elder does not feel their life has meaning and is wanted in service, they struggle with why to keep living.

My grandson, a Lakota spiritual guide and keeper of ceremonies, has reminded me that Elders are not the "best friend," the mother/father figure, the rescuer. Rather, they are as the North Star, a guiding light that points or illumines the way when needed. Especially, one of the ways this is done is by observing where deeper connection is needed to Nature and the Spirit world, offering guidance and practices of renewal that deepen and anchor that connectedness.

The Reverend Elder standing on her Spiral

ENDNOTES

1. Sue Monk Kidd, outstanding as one of women's favorite writers for her honesty and deep consideration of her story as she peers inside to reveal her truth. She wrote this memoir in 1996: *The Dance of the Dissident Daughter: A Woman's Journey from Christian Tradition to the Sacred Feminine.*

2. Angeles Arrien wrote and recorded *Living in Gratitude* in 2013.

3. Arnold van Gennep (1873-1957) published a monogram, *Rites of Passage* in 1908 and posthumously a book (1960) with the same title in which we are given liminality as the container for Rites of Passage. This is the key structure used for Passages: separation, the liminality of transformation, and incorporation. Victor and Edith Turner, as professors of anthropology, emphasized the "basic building blocks of culture" found in initiation rites, referencing van Gannep's fieldwork. These three were reason the archetype of change, initiation, has a language base.

4. Angeles Arrien, (1940-2014). One of her last offerings, *Living in Gratitude*, was widely published in 2013. I recommend everything by this earthy, indigenous professor, especially *The Second Half of Life: Opening the Eight Gates of Wisdom* (2005).

5. In 2002, Julia Cameron published a great gift for creative people, *The Artist's Way*. In it she called for a discipline to draw out or free up the artist in everyone, morning pages.

6. Michael Meade has phrases he could trademark. In 2013 and 2014, he held trainings that I attended. He referenced, *Betwixt & Between: Patterns of Masculine and Feminine Initiation* (1987), essays of the scholarly type for us to lean against. Personally I recommend Michael Meade's two books that weave magic all around and about Rites of Passage; *The Water of Life: Initiation* and the *Tempering of the Soul* (2006) and *Fate and Destiny: The Two Agreements of the Soul* (2010). www.mosaicvoices.org.

7. Brené Brown wrote two seminal books unpacking women's common sources for wounding—worthiness and shame—and healed by courage and vulnerability and wholeheartedness. She is generous in her platforms, find *The Gifts of Imperfection* (2010) and *Daring Greatly* (2012) in all variations and much more at www.brenebrown.com.

8. Maria Francesca Albergato my Swami, taught me that art like story and movement offers true and lasting healing. I was a participant in her research for her unpublished doctoral dissertation: *Transforming the Perception/Experience of Body Image in Women Traumatized by Breast Cancer* (2009).

9. Emily Hancock used solid research to demonstrate how identity development begins with the girl and circles back to her in Girl Within: *Recapture the Childhood Self, The Key to Female Identity* (1989).

10. Gail Burkett, Girls' *Ceremonies of Nine Passages* (Kindle Edition, 2014) was my entry into the world of e-books. Many more social experiments will follow. I will be happy to send you a PDF file of these two chapters of *Nine Passages* if you ask. This will be wrapped into the larger volume of *Nine Passages* in 2015.

11. Judith Duerk, *Circle of Stones* (1999). This is the book that caused my heart to quicken and my life to begin again with a new purpose, as an advocate for woman and girls. I am still haunted by the possibility of generations of women sitting together to share stories and find healing for themselves.

12. Kahlil Gibran, (1883-1931), *On Children* is widely quoted as are many parts of Gibran's epic poem, *The Prophet* (1923).

13. Larry Brendtro introduced me to *Circle of Courage* at a conference in 1997. I had a little sister who later became my foster daughter so I was learning about at-risk teens. In my research about risk, I determined that there are so many ways to trip up young people, most young people are at-risk. In psychology these are known as risk factors. I feel especially passionate about trainings for young women, we should withhold nothing and start with Circle of Courage through the Reclaiming Youth International website, https://www.reclaiming.com.

14. *Nine Passages* is designed for women with girls, for Elders and Mothers, to recognize maturity along a timeline and move through ritual ceremonies to acknowledge catalysts of change and transformation. *Nine Passages* may be especially useful as we cross previous thresholds to bring our acknowledgments up to date. When you see into others, this is a gift emerging in you. This is known as clairvoyance, the extra capacity for perception, and is a gift of Elders. We begin to see into others' behaviors in ways that please and also disturb us.

15. Dr. Clarissa Pinkola Estés' vast storytelling library can be found on www.SoundsTrue.com. I have a little history with my dear teacher, Dr. E. In 1995, I first read and re-read *Women Who Run with the Wolves: Myths and Stories of the Wild Woman Archetype* (1992) and felt like Dr. Estés encouraged my awakening. Then in 1997, newly enrolled at Union Institute for my doctoral studies, I found her dissertation on the library shelves and slept with it under my pillow. I have devoured all of the great works of Dr. E. over these two decades. One of her major recordings is *The Dangerous Old Woman*. I listened live as she recorded *The Late Bloomer* (2012). Also in 2012, I had the high privilege of being present for her ORIGINAL VOICE® training. Learn more at www.clarissapinkolaestes.com.

16. Carolyn Myss is a prolific contemporary teacher and healer, with many titles to her name. *Sacred Contracts: Awakening to Your Divine Potential* (2001) is one of three of her best sellers. Find much more here, www.myss.com.

17. Jean Shinoda Bolen, M.D. is probably most influential in women's ways for her wonderful book, *The Millionth Circle: How to Change Ourselves and The World* (1999) where she encourages women to gather together and become activists. *Goddesses in Older Women: Archetypes in Women over Fifty* (2001) is a major teaching on roots and archetypes.

18. Anne Lamott wrote *Bird by Bird: Some Instructions on Writing and Life* (1995) and I adopted her as a mentor because of her courage. Like most of her works that are autobiographical, *Help, Thanks, Wow: The Three Essential Prayers* (2012) is a gem filled with life's wisdoms.

19 Clarissa Pinkola Estés, PhD, published this master work, *Untie the Strong Woman: Blessed Mother's Immaculate Love for the Wild Soul* in 2011; inside are many powerful and useful prayers for women, like this Prayer for Traveling the Mother Roa.

20. A wonderfully deep and long training on Storytelling by Mary Alice Arthur and Amy Lenzo in which they hosted Michael Margolis as a Storytelling guest: Superhero Exercise. See more of Mary Alice at www.getsoaring.com and more of Amy Lenzo at www.wedialogue.com.

21. Byron Katie's phrase from her book, *Loving What Is: Four Questions That Can Change Your Life*, with Stephen Mitchell (2002) has served to upright me more than once. I also love *The Work* that rose from that, see www.byronkatie.com and www.thework.com.

22. Joseph W. Meeker is a play specialist, and eco-critic, a human ecologist, and my beloved mentor. He gave me an assignment to write my play history and I too became a play specialist. As third in a series, this work, *The Comedy of Survival: Literary Ecology and A Play Ethic* (1997) was published the year I met and asked Joe to be Core Faculty on my doctoral committee during my time at Union Institute.

Soul Stories

Nine Passages of Initiation

Soul Stories

ACKNOWLEDGEMENTS

Two darlings who breathed the same air as I for all these days of evolution and writing, thank you Kenny Olson and four legged, Rosie.

Teachers with broad shoulders for standing upon, helped me grow—Carol Gilligan, Clarissa Pinkola Estés, Angeles Arrien, Jean Shinoda Bolen, Joanna Macy, Sobonfu Some, Brené Brown, Michael Meade, Robert Bly, James Hillman, and Maya Angelou's poetic Soul. A few good Mentors influenced me profoundly because I was ready and wanted their help—Rick Medrick, Sharon Sweet, Joe Meeker, Susan Morgan, Alexandra Delis Abram; to these generous Souls, I bow in gratitude.

I needed to become an Elder with my squinty eyes to see the one true gift I have to offer the world. Looking inward, the wakened-self opened in little shaktipats from so many sacred Others, two-leggeds and four-leggeds. *Soul Stories* and the companion guide for Mothers and leaders, *Nine Passages*, are gifts from all of the women who ever crossed my path to help reveal myself to myself.

In the beginning of my awakening, Diana Eldridge held me while I went through fiery-watery depths in my own initiation. She is still holding. My Spirit has received support my entire life from Kathleen Bjorkman Wilson who is also still holding me. Kath offered her wilderness camp for the very first Rites of Passage in 2000 when I began to soar. Lauren Anschustegui and her mother Geri Brennan honored me with their open hearts and willing spirits. Geri left Lauren with me and Kath and Diana for a week in the wilderness; we dived in deep enough to birth this work and offer a transformative Passage experience for one lucky 12 year old girl.

A circle of 25 initiates for Womanhood Bloom, Deepening Womanhood, and Elder Encore stood with me around a Medicine Circle in the drizzling rain and we looked at our lives as a whole piece, that which was behind us and that which was before us. I thank these women for their gifts of trust and innocence, such a bond came through our long weekends together. Thank you to all of you who have held me tightly: Jolene Gail Daehlin, Debra Duwe, Debra Williams, Janet Dhaenens, Jane Sloan,

Kay Walker, Kit Kincaid, Hattie Goodman, Jennifer Ball, Karie Knoke, Becky Kemery and Swami Maria Albergato. I am deeply indebted to this Elder Circle for being my personal catalyst for change.

Over the past two decades, many women and I have held each other as we entered into deep and elongated conversations about Mothers and daughters, about women's changes, Moontime for us and our girls, and about initiations. In women's gatherings and sweat lodges Jo Davidson, Gayle Anderson, Nancy Smith, Chris Woods, Claire Walpole, and Colleen Mooney inspired trust and mutuality for the deepest of all connections. This is the Divine Feminine mirrored all across the land.

Lorene Wapotich and Arianna Husband spent hours and hours on the phone and in person to develop my thinking, especially when we planned the Middle Child ceremony. In a sacred circle, one Mother's question struck my heart: Kelley Ward, wanted an initiation for her little daughter but did not know how or what, but she knew why. Her daughter would have a deeper, more fulfilling life with ritual ceremonies to mark her path. That ceremony brought four Mothers, nine Grandmothers and five girls into ritual and play for the weekend. This is the one that makes all the other ceremonies possible and continuous.

Other ceremonies flushed with joy and teachings came through invitations from Jennie Ebrel, Rachel Rauch, Karen Porgoselski, Maya Goldbloom, Accalia Carter, and Anathea Woods. Mothers, beautiful Mothers have shared Passage ceremonies for their baby girls, Jani Davis, Cassie Dunn Faggion and Kathryn Eagen. I thank all beautiful Mothers for bringing granddaughters and grandsons through your wombs and into the world, oh my blessings.

For more than a year, Julia Zalesak, Kimberlie Gridley, and Sophia Rubedo came under my wing to discover who they were born to be. Initiation is the one transformative process that will reveal oneself to oneself. At the end of this pilgrimage, Janis Clark wrapped her wise arms around me and this work, staying through the birthing process like a doula. Laura Wahl, shining with her facets polished, created the art within the art. My Soul Sisters . . .

Our gang of 10 who have journeyed first with *Soul Stories* each indulged my imagination, mirrored mystery and wonder, and honored me with deep secrets: Kimberley Gridley, Julia Zalesak, and Paula Hickman as Sophia were first; Arianna Husband, Judith Lay, Janis Clark, Laura Wahl, and sisters, Kay Walker and Kit Kincaid completed ceremonies to deepen in the initiatory year through early 2016.

Please hug yourself for me, my dear blood-sisters, thank you for your love, your support, and all of the lessons: Janet Hatch, Debbie Davis, and Michele Burkett. Friends forever, Paula Johnson, Jean Herzel, and Marilyn McIntyre, I could not thrive without you.

My use of we includes these and many other women who have invited/allowed me the privilege to guide their personal pilgrimage to recover Rites of Passage. I am immeasurably wealthy. Already my tribe includes many endings, rest in peace. For end of life ceremonies, I thank my parents first for the opportunity to create quiet rituals for their passing,- and Lois Wythe and Becky Kemery. We are all growing old together and will cross over with very beautiful deaths in high ceremonial ritual.

©2015. Our Gratitude Goddess came to us in the intial design phase, because we wanted readers to pause and acknowledge a gift, a phrase, have an a-ha moment.

AUTHOR BIOGRAPHY

Gail Burkett is an advocate for women and girls creating ceremonial rituals for the important stages of development throughout life's long journey. Like an awakening, Gail's own journey began in her middle-of-life initiatory darkness. Nature's response to darkness is light, just as the psyche's response to a depression or trough is a challenge which invites a new peak ascent.

Following the cycles of Nature, watching women and girls in the culture, Gail chose the years between 8 and 12 as the most developmentally important to a girl's future as a woman. These years hold surprising revelations and challenges for girls and their Mothers. This was the subject of a Master's research project completed in 1998. The elongation of these thoughts led Gail to deeply explore where Women and Nature studies intersect. Emphasis on Rites of Passage ceremonies created by groups of women for young girls culminated in her first book, *Gifts from the Elders: Girls' Path to Womanhood.*

Gail teaches ritual by example and with simplicity; when combined into participatory rituals, a beautiful force is created with a root for re-membering. As a storyteller, she shares her own trials and asks questions to engage her audience in their personal story. This is how folk-psychology works. When we tell stories, we find the natural pattern of a circle which calls in Ancestor energy and honest sharing. Her beautiful way of questioning, handed down through the Nature connection communities, is most valuable for tracking one's life journey to Elderhood, as in *Soul Stories.*

With a PhD woven around Women and Nature Studies, conferred just after her 50th birthday, Gail is trained to find intersections of the fem-